GORBACHEV'S U.S.S.R.

Is Stalinism Dead?

NOT ADDED BY
UNIVERSITY OF MICHIGAN

GORBACHEV'S U.S.S.R.

Is Stalinism Dead?

A collection of essays in defense of socialist democracy

Edited by Carl Finamore
with contributions by

Esteban Volkov, Pierre Broué,
Susan Weissman, Nat Weinstein,
Paul Siegel, Ralph Schoenman,
Zbigniew Kowalewski, Gerry Foley,
Hayden Perry, and Carl Finamore

**Walnut Publishing Co., Inc.
San Francisco**

Gorbachev's U.S.S.R.: Is Stalinism Dead?
Edited by Carl Finamore
Copyright © 1989 by Walnut Publishing Co., Inc.
All rights reserved

Library of Congress Catalog Card Number: 89-51699

ISBN: 0-929405-04-8

Manufactured in the United States
First edition, 1989
Walnut Publishing Co., Inc.
3435 Army St., suite 308
San Francisco, CA 94110

About the Authors

Pierre Broué, author, noted historian, and director of the Leon Trotsky Institute in Paris, France. Broué's comprehensive biography of Trotsky has just been published. The work is based on previously sealed material in the Harvard archives and at Stanford University's Hoover Institute.

Carl Finamore, staff director since 1985 of the San Francisco-based Mobilization for Peace, Jobs and Justice, and a member of the National Committee of Socialist Action. Finamore traveled to Poland in 1982 while it was under martial law. In 1988, in collaboration with Polish Solidarnosc regional leader Zbigniew Kowalewski, he co-authored *Poland: Solidarnosc and the Struggle for Workers' Democracy*.

Gerry Foley, editor of *International Viewpoint*, an international review published in France under the auspices of the Fourth International. Foley is noted for his scholarly research on the question of oppressed nationalities. He is the author of *Rebellion in Ireland*.

Zbigniew Kowalewski, former regional leader of Polish Solidarnosc and author of *Give Us Back Our Factories: Solidarnosc and the Struggle for Workers' Self-Management in Poland*, among other works. Kowalewski is an authority on the national question in Eastern Europe.

Hayden Perry, author of *Everyday Life in Capitalist America: A Socialist Critique* and staffwriter for *Socialist Action* newspaper. Perry is a 50-year veteran of the Trotskyist movement.

Ralph Schoenman, past Executive Director of the Bertrand Russell Peace Foundation and past convenor of a nationwide symposium "American Workers and Artists for Polish Solidarity." Schoenman is the author of numerous books, including *Bertrand Russell: Philosopher of the Century*, *Prisoners of Israel*, and *The Hidden History of Zionism*.

Paul Siegel, Professor-Emeritus of English at Long Island University, New York. Siegel is a distinguished Shakespearean scholar. He is also co-chair of the Moscow Trials Campaign Committee, based in New York. This committee has organized a political campaign demanding the political rehabilitation of Leon Trotsky and other victims of Stalin's purges. Professor Siegel is the author of several books, including *Revolution and the 20th Century Novel* (1979), *Shakespeare's English and Roman History Plays: A Marxist Approach* (1986), and *The Meek and the Militant: Religion and Power Across the World* (1986).

Esteban (Sieva) Volkov, grandson of Leon Trotsky and leader of the international campaign to clear the name of Trotsky and other victims of Stalin's repression. At the age of 5, Sieva accompanied his mother, Zina, into forced exile from the Soviet Union. At the age of 12, after Zina's suicide, he went to live with the Trotsky household in Coyoacán, Mexico. Sieva was injured by gunfire in one of the first assassination attacks against Trotsky and was also witness to the last, fatal assault by one of Stalin's agents.

Nat Weinstein, Co-National Secretary of Socialist Action, a revolutionary socialist party in the United States in political solidarity with the Fourth International. Weinstein traveled to China immediately after the June 4, 1989, Tiananmen massacre to conduct a series of interviews and discussions with Chinese workers and students. He has written extensively on the subject of workers' democracy and socialism for the newspaper *Socialist Action*.

Susan Weissman, noted Sovietologist, author, and host/coordinator of the KPFK Radio (Los Angeles) nationally broadcast program "Portraits of the U.S.S.R." Weissman is a member of the editorial boards of numerous scholarly publications on Soviet studies and political affairs, including *Critique* and *Against the Current*. Her articles and lectures have included extensive research on the writings and ideas of noted Soviet revolutionary leader and author Victor Serge.

Contents

ACKNOWLEDGMENTS vii

INTRODUCTION ix

PART ONE –
The Meaning of Gorbachev's Reforms

The Failure of the New Soviet Reforms 1
   by Carl Finamore
The Crisis of Stalinism in the post-Stalin Era 25
   A Socialist Action Resolution

PART TWO –
Leon Trotsky: The Relevance of His Ideas

Trotsky's Grandson Salutes 50 Years of Struggle 55
   by Esteban Volkov
The Left Opposition and the U.S.S.R. Today 60
   by Paul Siegel
Prospects for Political Revolution in the U.S.S.R. 72
   by Nat Weinstein

PART THREE –
Trotskyists Return to the Soviet Union

A Trotskyist in Moscow 91
   by Pierre Broué
Trotsky's Grandson Returns to the Soviet Union 100
   An interview with Esteban Volkov

Delegation from Trotsky's Family Visits the U.S.S.R.   103
   by Carl Finamore

Greetings to Moscow People's Front Conference   112
   by Socialist Action and Delegation

Boris Yeltsin Rally Reveals Deep Ferment   114
   by Ralph Schoenman

Back in the U.S.S.R.   124
   by Susan Weissman

Moscow News Interviews Touring U.S. Trotskyists   144
   A Reprint

PART FOUR –
The Struggle of the Oppressed Nationalities

Introduction to Nationalist Struggle in the U.S.S.R.   149
   by Nat Weinstein

Gorbachev Faces Deep Crisis in the Baltic States   153
   by Hayden Perry

Gorbachev Uses Earthquake to Attack Armenians   156
   by Gerry Foley

Background to the Struggle in the Ukraine   161
   by Zbigniew Kowalewski

Acknowledgments

Gorbachev's U.S.S.R.: Is Stalinism Dead? is a collective effort by an international team of experienced revolutionary Marxists. Our collaboration on this book originated with a series of trips in 1989 to the Soviet Union. The visits produced volumes of information and insights—and filled us with great optimism for the future. We arrived in Moscow with suitcases laden with books, tape recorders, and cameras, most of which we placed in the hands of grateful Soviet political organizers. In exchange, we left Moscow with notepads filled with hastily scribbled observations, briefcases stuffed with leaflets, and dozens of cassette-taped interviews.

Our hosts in Moscow were from the People's Front and from the Socialist Initiative Group. They provided constant translation, continuous political discussion, creative tours of the streets and byways, and a crash course on the wonderfully efficient, though for me, perplexing Metro system. We owe a particular debt to Boris Kagarlitsky who made all the arrangements for our visit even as he was busy organizing the prefounding conference of the People's Front. Our interpreter was also from the Front. The young man was a 17-year-old political activist. He received permission from the People's Front to temporarily leave his important responsibilities as campaign organizer for the Front's candidate in the election for the Congress of People's Deputies. The candidate, Sergei Stankevich, subsequently won the election.

Our young translator spent 24 hours a day with us, keeping us up all hours of the night talking politics. Some of us hadn't done that in years. It was exhilarating for us and, I think, for him.

The major purpose of our trip to Moscow was to conduct discussions with political activists and government officials about the campaign to clear the names of Leon Trotsky and Victor Serge, the prominent Bolshevik anti-Stalinist fighter. This aspect of our tour was made possible through the political direction, comradely advice, and public sponsorship of Esteban (Sieva) Volkov, the grandson of Leon Trotsky. We deeply appreciate the commitment made by Sieva's family to the fight to clear the name of Leon Trotsky and other victims of Stalin's repression.

In particular, we must thank Palmira, Sieva's companion, who took our numerous late-night phone calls to Coyoacán, Mexico, always giving us her warm encouragement.

One contributor to this book deserves special mention. Pierre Broué traveled to Moscow in November 1988. To my knowledge, he was the first person since 1929 to speak before a public mass meeting in the U.S.S.R. as a supporter of Leon Trotsky and the anti-Stalinist struggle of the Bolshevik Left Opposition. The rousing reception he received inspired us to accelerate plans for our trip. Pierre provided names and phone numbers of leading political activists in Moscow. He also provided us with confidence and an inspiring example.

The idea of a trip to Moscow really began to attract support when the son of Victor Serge, Vlady Kibalchich, enthusiastically agreed to participate. Vlady's reputation as a prominent artist in Mexico and as a victim of Stalinist repression also served us well once we reached Moscow. As a young boy, Vlady was detained and interned for three years before he and his father were stripped of their Soviet citizenship and finally forced into exiled in 1936. Vlady's presence on our March 1989 tour to Moscow greatly enhanced the authority and respect we received.

But the project still required the active support of dozens of friends before it was possible for us to get on a plane to Moscow. We thank all of them heartily, especially Alexander Buchman, whose life-long commitment to the socialist cause brought him to our aid at a moment's notice.

While *Gorbachev's U.S.S.R.: Is Stalinism Dead?* is a genuinely collective effort, each contributor to this book is solely responsible for the contents of his or her individual article[s].

It was a pleasure to work with Alan Benjamin, whose highly respected political judgment, professional expertise, and calm demeanor made him especially well-suited to lead the team which compiled the manuscripts into a thoroughly readable and informative package. Alan was assisted by Paul Colvin, Sandy Doyle, May May Gong, Jeff Mackler, Hayden Perry, Joseph Ryan, and Michael Schreiber. All made valuable political suggestions with red pencil in hand. Their efforts are greatly appreciated.—C.F.

Introduction

When the Soviet Union launched the world's first space satellite in 1958, Sputnik entered overnight into the vocabulary of every language. Two new Russian words—*perestroika* and *glasnost*—have also rocketed to our attention, but with much more down-to-earth objectives.

Soviet economic, political, and social structures are being overhauled and, in some cases, wholly replaced. Communist Party (CPSU) General Secretary Mikhail Gorbachev has repeatedly, and often dramatically, initiated policies which appear to be radical breaks with the past. Why is this happening now?

The Soviet economy has not only stopped expanding but faces the very real possibility of sliding backwards. Agriculture output has virtually remained the same in the last 20 years, productivity of labor is dreadfully low, and the quality and quantity of Soviet products is a disgrace.

The Soviet Union has 280 million people and the world's richest deposits of oil, gas, and minerals. Yet the country never seemed able to achieve the heights of its potential.

The 27th CPSU Congress in 1986 took stock of the extensive waste and mismanagement of human and natural resources and promised a new course. It set incredibly ambitious goals.

Plans were made to double industrial output and national income by the year 2000. A pledge was made to solve the massive housing crunch by the year 2010. No one was going to wait the usual 20 years for an apartment again.

The government's report on "Guidelines for the Economic and Social Development of the U.S.S.R. for 1986-1990 and for the Period Ending in 2000" summarized these grandiose goals:

"The economic potential that will be created in the course of 15 years will approximately equal that which has been built throughout all the preceding years of Soviet power, and a long stride forward will be taken in building the material and technical basis of communism."

Similar promises were made 20 years ago in Poland. For example, every adult Pole was guaranteed a private apartment by the year 1985. But in 1989, young couples must still share an apartment with their parents for approximately 20 years before obtaining their own private dwelling. Mass disappointment often takes its revenge as evidenced by the rise of Solidarnosc, the 10 million-member independent union.

But it is not just the promise of tremendous expansion, or the dramatic consequences of its failure, which has fired people's imagination all over the world about events in the Soviet Union. Millions of people are also fascinated by the social evolution of the first great experiment in socialism. People are asking the question: Has socialism failed and is the Soviet Union turning toward capitalist-type reforms to recover its balance?

Of course, the capitalist news media gloats over this situation. They have been saying all along that socialism doesn't work and now they appear to have been proven right.

The authors of the essays in this book take a different point of view. They are supporters of the Russian Revolution but believe that its original socialist goals were corrupted by the emergence of a privileged Stalinist bureaucracy which still rules today.

Seventy years ago, the 1917 Russian Revolution changed the course of world history. A backward, peasant-based country suddenly erupted with a series of two revolutions in a space of nine months. The February 1917 revolution toppled the Czar, establishing a rather unstable bourgeois government. Only several months later, in November, the socialist revolution installed the Soviet of Workers, Peasants, and Soldiers into power.

The February bourgeois government led by Alexander F. Kerensky never attained exclusive authority and was forced to share power with the soviets (councils), a new form of workers' democracy first developed during a powerful anti-Czarist struggle in 1905.

The soviets emerged throughout Russia in the months leading up to the 1917 insurrection. They were made up of elected delegates from mass organizations representing millions of workers, peasants, and soldiers.

V.I. Lenin, leader of the Russian Revolution, described soviet democracy as "first in this: that the electorate comprises the toiling and exploited masses—that the bourgeoisie is excluded. Secondly, in this: that all bureaucratic formalities and limitations of elections are done away with—that the masses themselves determine the order and the time of elections and with complete freedom of recall of elected officials. Thirdly, that the best possible mass organization of the vanguard of the toilers—of the industrial proletariat—is formed, enabling them to direct the exploited masses, to attract them to active participation in political life, to train them politically through their own experience, that in this way a beginning has been made for the first time actually to get the whole population to learn how to engage and to begin managing."[1]

After April 1917, the Bolshevik Party (later to change its name to the CPSU) promoted the idea of "All Power to the Soviets." This reflected their view that a workers' and peasants' government should be formed, a government without capitalists. The Menshevik and Socialist Revolutionary majority inside the soviet argued for maintaining capitalist economic relations and, therefore, continually deferred to the bourgeois government.

The Menshevik and Socialist Revolutionary party leaderships consistently acted to dilute the power of the soviet. This meant that Kerensky's capitalist government had a free hand to pursue the imperialist World War I, which took an incredibly large toll on the Russian people. The army was ill-equipped and poorly led. The peasant soldiers were straining to return home to harvest their crops rotting in the fields. The workers in the city were chafing at the long hours and low pay in the factories.

And, of course, it was these two classes who were pushed to the front as cannon fodder. Inevitably, these circumstances led to a social explosion: riots, demonstrations, and, eventually, calls for an end to the war, for bread, and for land to the peasants.

The Bolshevik Party grew as the crisis deepened. The membership of 24,000 in March 1917 surged to 350,000 in October, when party leader Leon Trotsky took the stage of the soviet in the capital city of Petrograd to announce his acceptance of the post of chairman.

Trotsky said: "We are certain that the work of the new Presidium will be accompanied by a new rise in the development of the revolution. We belong to different parties and have our own work to conduct, but in directing the work of the Petrograd Soviet we will observe the individual rights and complete freedom of all fractions: The arm of the Presidium will never be used to stifle a minority."[2]

This Bolshevik appeal for unity of the working class parties marked the beginning of the Russian Revolution, culminating in a brief insurrection several weeks later that easily dispersed the crumbling remnants of the capitalist government. The transformation from bourgeois to prole-

---

1. V.I. Lenin, *The Soviets at Work* (New York: Rand School of Social Research, 1919), p. 30.
2. A. Rabinowitch, *The Bolsheviks Come to Power* (New York: Norton, 1978), p. 189.

tarian government was relatively peaceful due to the disproportionate relationship of forces favoring the revolution.

"Supported by the overwhelming majority of the workers, soldiers, and peasants, and basing itself on the victorious insurrection of the workers and the garrison of Petrograd, the congress hereby resolves to take governmental power into its own hands."[3]

The private, semi-feudal landed estates were confiscated and given to the peasants. The capitalist-owned factories, mines, and mills were expropriated and placed under the control of the workers. Land to the peasants, workers' control of industry, and an immediate declaration of peace were the first liberating decrees of the new Soviet government. This was an unprecedented and historic moment for all humanity.

The Bolsheviks under V.I. Lenin and Leon Trotsky repeatedly emphasized the critical role of mass organizations through which the majority could actively participate in government. Lenin's theses on democracy were adopted by the First Congress of the Communist International in 1919.

The report stated that "genuine democracy . . . is possible only . . . by enlisting the mass organizations of the working people in constant and unfailing participation in the administration of the state."

For the first time in history, the workers, peasants, and soldiers—the overwhelming majority of the population—controlled the government. In fact, the Bolshevik program went further. It called for the workers and peasants to *be* the government.

"It gives those who were formerly oppressed," Lenin said, "the chance to straighten their backs and, to take the whole government of the country, the whole administration of the economy, the whole management of production, into their own hands."

Several parties in bitter opposition to the Bolsheviks functioned in the soviets. They participated in soviet elections, circulated their press, and organized meetings and demonstrations. After the revolution, their rights were fully guaranteed. In fact, the Bolsheviks actively solicited the participation of Soviet opposition parties in the government immediately after the insurrection. But only a small left-wing section of the Socialist Revolutionary Party agreed for a brief period to join. The other parties took up arms against the revolution. As a result, they were outlawed.

---

3. V.I. Lenin, *To All Workers, Soldiers, and Peasants,* November 1917 manifesto passed by the All-Russian Congress of Soviets which legitimized soviet power.

The ensuing civil war, promoted by the invasion of 14 imperialist countries, including the United States, not only imposed severe physical hardships on the Soviet population, but also gravely altered the political course charted by the Bolsheviks.

The war-ravaged economy plunged into a huge abyss. Famine spread. But the social vision of the working class and the desire of the peasants for land still burned bright enough to snuff out the counterrevolution by 1921.

Yet, the toll was excruciatingly painful. Millions of people were killed, including many of the best revolutionary veterans. The CPSU itself underwent deep changes. By 1923, the party was mostly composed of new recruits; 90 percent of its membership joining after the revolution.

Tremendous disruption was also caused by retreating imperialist armies which flooded mines, tore up railroad ties, and burned fields. But even after their armies were driven from Soviet territory, the European and American capitalists were to deal yet another final blow to the revolution. A reign of terror against the "Bolshevik menace" was unleashed against the working class in most of the major countries of the world. The impending German revolution, for example, was drowned in blood. Its two luminous figures, Rosa Luxemburg and Karl Liebnecht, were assassinated by the police of the Social Democratic government.

The Russian Revolution was isolated internationally. This, coupled with the devastating civil war, set the stage for a conservative mood to develop among the exhausted soviet masses. Under these conditions, Josef Stalin consolidated his power.

The perspective of promoting revolution abroad was set aside. A domestic policy of "enriching" yourself was instituted by Stalin and Nikolai Bukharin as a substitute for proletarian internationalism.

These policies represented a complete rupture with Bolshevik tradition. The party was destroyed, its internal democracy shattered, its historic program overturned. It was replaced by a corrupt, bureaucratic, and repressive political machine which usurped power from the soviets. The direct rule of the workers and peasants was ended. The government of soviets became a mere rubber stamp for Stalin's reactionary policies. "It was not he who created the machine," Trotsky wrote of Stalin, "but the machine that created him."

Soviet authorities now acknowledge that over 20 million were killed during the Stalin era, including almost all the central leaders of the 1917 revolution. (Marxist historian Roy Medvedev's estimate is 40 million killed.) This statistic alone should give pause to those who consider the Stalinist dictatorship to be the logical outgrowth of Leninism and Bolshevism. Stalin killed because he could not co-exist with the long-established traditions of party and soviet democracy.

The gulf between "Bolshevism and Stalinism [is] not simply a bloody line but a whole river of blood," observed Trotsky several years before he was also assassinated by Stalin's agent in Coyoacán, Mexico, in 1940.

Trotsky commented that democracy "narrowed in proportion as difficulties increased. In the beginning, the party had wished and hoped to preserve freedom of political struggle within the framework of the Soviets. The civil war introduced stern amendments to this calculation."[4] Trotsky stressed that the leaders of the revolution considered any measures in conflict with soviet democracy "not as a principle, but as an episodic act of self-defense."

As civil-war induced famine spread across the Soviet Union in 1921, Lenin and Trotsky were forced to support severe restrictions on the highly valued party democracy. There was a ban on organizing internal party groupings apart from the democratically elected leadership of the CPSU.

Trotsky reports that these steps were "again regarded as an exceptional measure to be abandoned at the first serious improvement in the situation . . . lest it lead to a strangling of the inner life of the party."

But, unfortunately, temporary measures taken in self-defense perfectly suited the needs of the emerging privileged layer to silence all dissent. To this day, even with the much-heralded *glasnost*, factions and tendencies are strictly prohibited in the CPSU.

Lenin's last political act before he died was an offer to form a bloc with Trotsky against the developing bureaucratic deformations in the CPSU and soviets. Trotsky continued this fight until he was murdered by an assassin carrying out Stalin's orders. The assassin was later awarded the Order of the Red Flag by the Soviet government.

What happened to the great promise of 1917 and to the hopes that inspired millions across the world? How did Stalin and a privileged bureaucracy develop? Was it inevitable? Leon Trotsky answers these and other questions in his classic exposé of Stalinism, *The Revolution Betrayed*, where he demonstrates that Stalinism represents the negation of Leninism and revolutionary Marxism. In full agreement with that assessment, *Gorbachev's U.S.S.R.: Is Stalinism Dead?* analyzes current events against the backdrop of the struggle for socialist democracy

---

4. Leon Trotsky, *Revolution Betrayed* (New York: Merit Publishers, 1965), p. 96.

fought out several decades earlier by the original Bolshevik Left Opposition to Stalin.

Author Paul Siegel's essay, for example, traces the links between the historic fight of the Bolshevik Left Opposition to the mass opposition movements today. Siegel explains why the major planks in the platform of the Trotskyist opposition are essential ingredients of the political revolution required to overturn the existing hardened Stalinist bureaucracy led today by Gorbachev.

Marxist scholar and Trotsky biographer Pierre Broué expands on this theme. He describes his own personal experience in 1988 in Moscow with the new generation of fighters in the Soviet Union, as well as his contact with veterans from the original anti-Stalinist opposition. Broué describes what it was like to be the first person in 60 years to openly announce support for the Trotskyist anti-bureaucratic struggle at a public mass meeting in the U.S.S.R.

Socialist Action Co-National Secretary Nat Weinstein contributes to the discussion of how the political revolution will develop in the Soviet Union from the unique vantage point of his recent visit to China. The Chinese bureaucrats' experiment with *perestroika* reforms goes back 10 years. These policies provoked a mass rebellion in the spring of 1989 and offer many valuable comparisons with Gorbachev's reforms.

The significance of Trotsky's ideas and the revolutionary concept that socialism and democracy are inseparable is presented in a speech by Esteban Volkov, Leon Trotsky's grandson. Volkov originally addressed his remarks to a rally sponsored by the U.S. Trotskyist party Socialist Action in celebration of the 50th anniversary of the founding of the Fourth International. Trotsky formed the Fourth International in 1938 as a new world party of socialist revolution after Stalin's policies destroyed the revolutionary principles of the Third International established by Lenin and the Bolsheviks in 1919. Volkov's speech is a dramatic, personal account of a life-long association with these ideas. As a young boy of 12, he was injured in one of the assassination attempts against Trotsky.

Other essays in this book examine the origins, goals, and effects of the Gorbachev-sponsored reforms underway in the Soviet Union. The authors respond to the question, "Did Stalinism die with Stalin?"

They answer that the bureaucratic, totalitarian machine still rules. Its parts have been overhauled, some replaced, others removed, but it still grinds on.

The most innovative manager of all, Mikhail Gorbachev, has appeared on the scene because some serious repairs are required. Just holding a steady course, as former Premier Leonid Brezhnev did several years ago, isn't enough. The Soviet economy has come to a serious impasse.

As a result, other reformers besides Gorbachev have begun to appear from within the bureaucracy. These CPSU "radicals" are quite aware of the volatile mood of the population and, therefore, sometimes politically differentiate themselves from official government policy. But none of the reformers inside the CPSU can possibly address the basic problem—eliminating the privileged CPSU apparatus.

Ralph Schoenman, author and former secretary of the Bertrand Russell Peace Foundation, describes the role of the most prominent maverick in the CPSU, the popular People's Congress Deputy Boris Yeltsin. Schoenman was present during a mass pre-election meeting for Yeltsin in March 1989. He describes what occurred after the rally was taken over by the militant audience, who forthrightly presented demands going far beyond Yeltsin's plans.

Despite very skillful political maneuvers, neither Gorbachev nor any section of the CPSU can claim full control of the situation. As in China, disappointment over the failure of the reforms will only turn up the heat. It has already happened. The miners' strike of 500,000 in July 1989 was no fluke.

The strike threatened to paralyze the country, proving once again that workers have not lost any of their power and are now even beginning to regain their political will.

This dream is Gorbachev's nightmare. It is soon to become a reality. There will be more strikes and protests because the economic reforms actually aggravate the crisis. *Perestroika* economic reforms increase social differentiation, increase prices, and increase unemployment. Susan Weissman's article in this book covers this aspect of the reforms quite extensively.

Weissman explains how Gorbachev's reforms are designed to attract the intellectuals, technocrats, and highly skilled workers rather than the mass of working people who are, in fact, expected to pay the cost of the reforms.

Major mass struggles have become a regular feature of Soviet political life. Many are the product of deeply felt and profoundly revolutionary nationalist sentiment, long suppressed under Stalin. The Baltic countries of Latvia, Lithuania, and Estonia are demanding greater autonomy and even independence. These highly productive regions want an end to Moscow's discriminatory control over their economy. They want freedom for their language, culture, and national customs.

Millions of people in the 14 non-Russian republics believe that some degree of political independence is a precondition for economic justice.

Decades of Stalinist bureaucratic rule has propelled this issue to the fore.

The national question deserves serious consideration by anyone interested in Soviet politics. It is the single-most burning issue fueling the anti-bureaucratic struggle and is extensively covered by writers Hayden Perry, Gerry Foley, and Zbigniew Kowalewski. Perry explains the historical background to the national disputes in the Baltic region while Foley and Kowalewski analyze the national question in Armenia and the Ukraine.

Gorbachev's U.S.S.R.: Is Stalinism Dead? begins with two articles which give a comprehensive overview of the current political and economic situation in the Soviet Union. Carl Finamore's article describes why the economic and democratic reforms have largely failed. He also predicts continued growth of the mass opposition movement with greater participation of the working class.

The second article in the first chapter was prepared by Socialist Action, a party which considers democracy and mass participation in government an absolute precondition for the development of socialism. Socialist Action traces its roots to the early Bolshevik fighters who gave their lives in the fight against Stalinist degeneration of these principles.

There is a final piece of information about this book which should be of interest to readers. There are several articles from participants in a delegation which traveled to the Soviet Union in March 1989 on behalf of the families of Leon Trotsky and Victor Serge. A leading Left Oppositionist, Serge was exiled by Stalin in 1936. The delegation from the family, of which I was a member, also included Susan Weissman, Paul Siegel, Ralph Schoenman, and Vlady Kibalchich, son of Victor Serge.

Our primary task in Moscow was to deliver a letter from Trotsky's relatives asking that his name be cleared and that all his writings be published. It was the first time that representatives of Trotsky's family returned to the Soviet Union since 1929.

We arranged a meeting with Otto Latsis, a Central Committee member of the CPSU and deputy editor of *Kommunist*, the theoretical organ of the CPSU. Latsis accepted the letter and informed our delegation that the matter would be discussed by the Central Committee. We haven't heard anything further at this point.

We also met with a wide range of dissidents in the Peoples' Front of Moscow and with members of Memorial, a group initiated by victims of Stalin's terror. People were interested, even eager, to speak with us.

We had discussions with two candidates who were running for the Congress of People's Deputies—Marxist historian, author, and dissident

Roy Medvedev, and People's Front leader Sergei Stankevich. Both won their races and are now Congress Deputies.

We were interviewed by several newspapers such as *Moscow News, Komsomolskaya Pravda*, a Moscow University newspaper, a Moscow CPSU youth paper, a Moscow region newspaper, and a Baltic region newspaper.

Our most memorable visit was with Nadezhda Joffe, an original member of the Left Opposition and daughter of Bolshevik leader Adolf Joffe. In 1927, Adolf Joffe committed suicide as a final act of political protest against the growing Stalinist bureaucratic machine, which refused his request for medical treatment abroad.

Nadezhda, herself, was imprisoned three times, her husband shot, and her children sent to labor camp orphanages. Nadezhda was 82 years young when we met her.

She gave us a spirited interview describing the high goals and motivations of her generation. "Lenin and Trotsky," she said, "conceived of the revolution as the highest intellectual, cultural, and social achievement in history." "It was Stalin," Nadezhda said with conviction, "who destroyed the Bolshevik Party and tradition in order to impose his dictatorship."

This book was inspired by our exhilarating experience in Moscow. We met with the older generation and the young fighters, each reaching out to link their hands to renew the struggle for socialist democracy so long suppressed and too long postponed.

The Soviet Union gave birth to the greatest revolution of all time in 1917. It seemed to all of us that its rebirth was destined to make an even greater impact. This book is dedicated to that purpose.

Carl Finamore
San Francisco, Calif.
Sept. 12, 1989.

PART ONE

The Meaning of Gorbachev's Reforms

The Failure of the New Soviet Reforms

By CARL FINAMORE

Soviet President Mikhail Gorbachev's economic program is in big trouble. While he is extremely popular among Western capitalists eager to make a quick buck through new investment opportunities, Gorbachev is getting considerably less rave reviews at home.

"Society will be destabilized" if the economy does not improve within the next two years, said Leonid Abalkin, deputy prime minister. Other warnings are even more dire. People's Congress deputy and economist Vladimir Tikhonov predicted "famine in the very near future" unless radical changes are made.[1]

Only four months earlier, Abalkin was far more relaxed about the pace of reforms. He was saying that it would take until 1995 before they would achieve any significant results. He told a press conference at the time that, "The important thing to know is, when will people, sitting around their kitchen tables, finally be able to say: 'Oh, life is much better now than it was.' I think this will happen only by 1995, and we will be reaping the first palpable changes by then."[2]

Gorbachev was also preaching patience. He opposed the idea of importing large amounts of scarce consumer goods. If anything is imported, he implied in a televised speech, it should be the equipment to manufacture consumer goods.

This cautious approach to reforms was reversed in less than four months. By April 1989 Abalkin was forecasting serious social unrest and Gorbachev was announcing more than a 15 percent increase in scheduled purchases of foreign consumer goods ranging from leather shoes, toothpaste, cassette tapes, and pantyhose. The total bill was 5 billion rubles for what had been previously considered by Gorbachev as "utterly irresponsible."

Why the Turnaround? The March 26, 1989, national elections. These

---

Carl Finamore is a member of the National Committee of Socialist Action. He coordinated the March 1989 trip to Moscow by a delegation representing the families of Leon Trotsky and Victor Serge.

elections recorded humiliating defeats for large numbers of government and Communist Party (CPSU) representatives and sent a shock wave throughout the apparatus. Despite numerous obstacles, millions of people participated in pre-election political activity. This took the bureaucrats by complete surprise and threw them off balance.

Previous economic timetables were revised. The government used its checkbook to buy some time. It sought to defuse the situation before it reached the point of explosion—and this could only be done with actions, not words.The gradual elimination of government food subsidies scheduled for 1989 was postponed for two years. These government subsidies amount to $91 billion and are a significant benefit for the population. Milk, egg, and bread prices, for example, have hardly changed in 20 years.

In his inaugural speech as president, Gorbachev also called for measures to improve the income of 40 million Soviet citizens who live below the poverty line. He even warned against calls to "turn on full-blast the mechanism of a market economy."

"We don't agree with this approach," he said. "It would immediately explode the whole social situation and violate all processes in the country."[3]

Gorbachev realizes that his pet project of market reforms has already antagonized large sections of the population and is mindful of public resentments against the entrepreneurs who have become rich in private business.

The private cooperatives now charge about three times as much for their products as state enterprises and about five times as much for their services according to a recent study by Moscow's Institute of Sociology. Two-thirds of the Muscovites queried in the study also said they cannot afford cooperative prices.[4]

The privileged bureaucrats are in a better position to wait five or six years for improvements. The average Soviet citizen must endure long lines and empty shelves every day. A woman wrote a letter to the government newspaper *Izvestia* complaining that she waited five hours in line for three bars of soap and three tubes of toothpaste. "We are patient people, that's known," she wrote. "But do they need to test the limits of our patience so thoroughly and for so long?"

Economist Nikolai Petrakov described the government's dilemma: "How can you explain that to an ordinary citizen who heard the same thing from [Leonid I.] Brezhnev and before that from [Nikita S.] Khrushchev, that soon everything will be all right?"

It's Not a Sin to be Rich

Reaction to Gorbachev's reforms among pro-capitalist observers is quite different from that of the average Soviet citizen. A *Wall Street Journal* correspondent suggested, for example, that the CPSU Central Committee pass a resolution making "it socially, politically and legally acceptable to become rich. Every Soviet citizen has the inalienable right to make as much money as he or she can."[5]

This U.S. journalist is not alone. Many within the U.S.S.R. are also pushing the "get-rich-quick" spirit. Andrei Konovalov said that "there is a stereotype that makes it a virtue to do away with the rich. We still have the psychological tendencies of the poor." Mr. Konovalov is chairman of the Moscow Union of Cooperatives, the socialist-sounding term given to private establishments.

These seeds are finding fertile ground. In January 1988 there were 13,921 cooperatives employing 155,800 people. "In January 1989, with a comprehensive law to encourage them, 77,548 cooperatives employed 1.4 million."[6]

Others in government relish the "get-rich" theme. One new millionaire was included by Gorbachev on the slate of 100 CPSU deputies in the Congress. Politburo member Vadim Medvedev went even further, stating that "the current experimentation with cooperative [private] ownership and renting property to farmers and small entrepreneurs should be expanded to heavy industry."[7]

Social Differentiation Accelerates

Under the Bolsheviks, free market-type economic reforms were successfully introduced to fill the large gaps in the war-torn planned economy. But these reforms were envisaged as being under the strict accounting and control of the working class.

The bureaucratically organized market reforms under Gorbachev will give free rein to profit-seekers. A December 1988 decision by the Council of Ministers gave all Soviet enterprises the right to engage in direct trade with foreign firms. These firms number around 45,000.

Previously, this right had been exercised exclusively by the government. As it stands now, the government only imposes certain import/export restrictions which deal with "regulating supply and demand on the home market." But the government will have a very difficult time regulating thousands of private joint ventures and entrepreneurs, all of whom are most interested in exporting their products to the profitable foreign market. Long waiting lines and scarcity of mass consumer items will continue to grow as a result.

A thriving black market flourishes under these condition. These illegal operations fill huge holes in the economy. The Ministry of Internal Affairs estimates that two-thirds of the raw material necessary for Moscow's everyday services could be obtained only for a bribe.[8] With the market reforms, these profiteers will be able to charge their outrageous prices legally.

Perestroika market reforms will mean more price hikes, more unemployment, and more misery for the working class. Tatyana Koryangina, head of the Economic Research Institute under the U.S.S.R. State Planning Committee, argues that "if there are to be big changes, social losses are inevitable."

She concedes that unemployment will be the result because "the market legalizes the difference in incomes and links them with labor input." She also admits that unemployment compensation only lasts "two or three months' wages, then the law stipulates nothing."[9]

It is officially estimated that "no fewer than 16 million" people will be unemployed over the next 12 years.[10]

Sitting from her privileged position, Koryangina has no problem adding that, "We must give up the dogmas about 'completely free welfare.'" The response from the average Soviet citizen, however, is completely different. This is especially true of those people who have directly experienced the economic reforms.

"He is a capitalist, every inch of him," was the unanimous reaction told to a *Moscow News* interviewer by an 11-women team of gardeners working on a farm cooperative in Novosibirsk. They were referring to the owner of the cooperative. "Who wants a type like that around here? Last year they promised us the moon: 'Do a good job of it and we'll pay you premiums.' We worked like mad, and then they waved a paper at our face claiming that wages had been growing faster than efficiency. What does that mean to us?"

How is the Pie Divided?

The huge privileged bureaucracy comprises the largest drain on the Soviet economy. It has grown to include tens of millions. Leon Trotsky considered its size even in the 1930s to include as many as 40 million people.

The U.S.S.R. has "one of the world's highest figures for state management," reported Alexander Zaichenko, a senior researcher at the Institute of the USA and Canada. In 1987, "we spent on management (plus defense) 29 percent, or 239 billion rubles." [The 1989 Congress of People's Deputies reported that defense spending was 77 billion rubles, or 9 percent of GNP. Therefore, we can conclude that approximately 20 percent of GNP is spent on management.]

Gorbachev recognizes that the sheer size of the bureaucracy has gotten out of control. There are, for example, 14 million farmworkers in the Soviet Union, but 4 million of them are managers or bureaucrats of some form.[11]

Another example is the farm-management system of Gosagroprom, a super-ministry initiated—but later abolished—by Gorbachev. An order issued by the Gosagroprom chairman passed through 32 stages before it reached the farm.

This bungling inefficiency produces deep resentment in the average citizen. Gorbachev is taking steps to prune the tree. The new Chairman of the U.S.S.R. Council of Ministers stated to the 1989 Supreme Soviet that there would be a sharp cut, by nearly a third, in the number of federal ministries.

It is not clear, however, whether this will lead to a reduction in the actual size of the bureaucracy since many functions of these ministries will simply be shifted to other departments. What is really needed is an inspection by independent committees of the workers, peasants, and farm workers to determine which of these "functions" are needed by society.

Mismanagement accounts for incredible holes in the economy, which the bureaucracy then seeks to fill by making more holes. Managers fulfill the economic plan targets at all costs in order to make themselves look good and to earn bonuses. In many cases this means fraudulently inflating production figures. This has created a fictitious economy where numbers, goals, and targets are seldom taken seriously.

This sad state of affairs prompted one writer to ask rhetorically: "Isn't it because of this that we are now starting to admit bitterly that about 40 percent of our gross social product is not a commodity, but a repeat account of what has already been manufactured and accounted for."[12]

Clearly, decades of bureaucratic rule has resulted in the Soviet people receiving far less than a fair share of return from their labor, especially after a big 20 percent chunk of the social surplus is siphoned off by the "managers."

Still, the government makes the preposterous claim that Soviet workers and peasants consume too much of the total social product. In fact, far less of the social product returns to the population in the form of consumer items than in other countries.

In the U.S.S.R., consumers absorbed 41 percent of the total GNP in 1987. In other developed countries, the figure is between 60 percent to

70 percent. In the United States it is 66 percent.

Neither is the comparison between low prices in the Soviet Union and high prices in the United States necessarily an accurate indication of greater social benefits. More important than the price is the amount of labor time it takes a worker to earn the purchase price of products. Here, the cost of bureaucratic mismanagement is dearly paid by the consumer. For example, a Soviet citizen must work 10 times longer than an American to purchase one pound of meat.[13]

Food First

Soviet agriculture is the biggest disappointment and most explosive issue for Gorbachev and his predecessors. It is a very grim story. In nine of the last 12 five-year economic periods, the growth of farm output has been insignificant or negative. The last really successful five-year period ended in 1970.

This has created a whole host of problems. The wide expanse of agricultural land should be earning the critically needed foreign currency cash from exports. Instead, the Soviet Union must import grain and other food products. And still, people in the Soviet Union eat almost two-thirds less meat than North Americans.

Shortages of basic consumer items and scarce food supplies is an everyday fact of life. Sugar is being rationed in Moscow for the first time since World War II. Government economist Otto Latsis reported that of the 211 basic food products ranked by a Moscow research institute, only 23 were readily available.[14]

With billions of unspent rubles being hoarded because there are not enough consumer products to purchase, the Soviet people are bursting with pent-up anger, frustration and—purchasing power. With an estimated 300 billion rubles sitting in savings banks and another 90 billion stashed under mattresses, these rubles effectively increase the inflation rate rather than boost commercial sales.

What's the problem with farm production? It's not primarily the result of low productivity of the farm workers. The problem is no different than that which plagues the cities—there is little incentive to produce when there is a scarcity of quality consumer goods available in exchange. And these shortages are particularly acute in the countryside.

In addition, there is the ever-present problem of mismanagement. Each competing bureaucratic sector jealously guards its own nest, refusing to abide by the needs of the overall economic plan.

For example, about one-third of farm produce rots before it reaches the market. Poor road conditions and insufficient transport and refrigeration units are mostly responsible. These problems reflect the extreme imbalances in state investments because of overall lack of national democratic control over economic decisions.

One ministry invests billions of rubles in planting vegetables while another ministry fails to produce sufficient vehicles to transport the high yield, which then invariably wastes away in storage bins.

Gorbachev's solution to the agrarian problem is to do away with the collective farms and instill the profit motive into the Soviet farm economy. This, however, is no solution at all. The profit motive in agriculture runs the same risks as those already incurred in industry.

Planting may very well shift away from inexpensive foods toward highly priced specialty crops. And if private peasants are allowed to grow crops specifically for more profitable foreign markets, a serious food shortage could develop. A food shortage is not idle speculation. It is, in fact, exactly what occurred in Soviet agriculture in the 1920s under similar conditions.

Interestingly, Gorbachev's agricultural program is modeled on views adopted by Josef Stalin and Nikolai Bukharin in the 1920s—policies which, in fact, account for the tragic roots of Soviet farming.

The Roots of Gorbachev's Food Policy

Since coming to power in 1985, Soviet leader Mikhail Gorbachev has regularly leaned on the early record of the Bolsheviks for his support, hoping that it will provide the necessary historical and theoretical precedents for his current policies. While shoveling more dirt on Stalin's political grave, Gorbachev has resurrected the popular Bolshevik leader, Bukharin, who was the chief architect of Stalin's economic policies from 1923 to 1928.

Bukharin and Stalin claimed to base their policies on the New Economic Policy (NEP), which the Bolsheviks adopted in 1921. This is not completely accurate. Though some elements were similar, the strategy pursued from 1923 to 1928 was completely opposed to that of the Bolshevik Party under Lenin and Trotsky.

Stalin's and Bukharin's reactionary approach flowed from their defeatist orientation of building "socialism in one country." Lenin and Trotsky maintained the traditional Bolshevik theory of linking the fate of the first workers' state to the advance of the world revolution. The early Bolsheviks stressed the need for socialist revolutions in every country, especially Germany. It was considered self-evident that the young and economically backward Soviet republic could only survive with financial credit, raw materials, and tens of thousands of skilled workers supplied by other victorious revolutions.

Non-exploitative international economic relationships would have eliminated the capitalist "world market" profit criterion for trade. A new trade basis between countries would develop commensurate with the expansion of productive capacity, eventually leading to a generalized system of planned economy in distribution as well as production.

But these post-World War I revolutions failed. The young Soviet republic was isolated and on the verge of economic collapse after four years of imperialist armed intervention.

In 1921, immediately after the civil war, factory production was one-fifth of the pre-war level. The collapse of productive forces surpassed anything history had ever seen. A devastating chain reaction took effect. The peasants refused to supply food to the cities because factories were not producing commercial products in exchange. They hid their harvested crops, saving them for a better day.

Under civil-war pressures, the government was forced to militarily requisition agricultural products. But that "military communism" policy had to stop when the war ended.

The NEP thus began in 1921. It utilized pre-revolution production incentives such as supply and demand and traditional money payments. Trade between the city and countryside was re-established on this basis. In this sense, Lenin and Trotsky supported the NEP as a necessary "retreat."

Trotsky describes the objectives of the NEP as quite simple: "Industry should supply the rural districts with necessary goods at such prices as would enable the state to forego forcible collection of the products of peasant labor."

But a major dispute soon broke out in 1923, with Trotsky on one side and Bukharin and Stalin on the other. It involved defining the exact character of production incentives. This may appear to have been a rather academic discussion. It wasn't. The results radically altered the future course of the Soviet Union, with many of the same issues resurfacing today.

Trotsky urged a steady increase in industrial growth to supply the peasants with farm equipment and consumer items to serve as necessary production incentives. He correctly predicted that this relationship was the firmest basis for closing the "scissors," a reference to the ever-widening social gap between the city and country.

Industrial expansion, Trotsky argued, would be financed by charging peasants a higher price for commercial goods and paying them less for their agricultural stocks. This unequal exchange—or "borrowing"—

from the peasants was absolutely necessary in order to rebuild the devastated economy. Of course, the price differentials could not be excessive. Trotsky points out that, "Too heavy 'forced loans' of products, however, would destroy the stimulus . . . [for peasant] labor."

Stalin and Bukharin had a completely different approach—one which is remarkably similar to today's *perestroika* reforms. They introduced capitalist profit incentives to increase farm production. This only aggravated the imbalance between city and country, while intensifying the oppression of poor peasants by rich landowners, or kulaks.

Bukharin told the peasants to "get rich." Both he and Stalin encouraged the kulaks to let supply and demand market mechanisms exclusively determine the price of their products. Unfortunately, a large number took this advice seriously. A broad layer of rich peasants and middlemen, the "NEP-men," developed.

Millions of peasants refused to sell their grain to the government unless prices were continually raised. This price-gouging siphoned away scarce government capital needed to build up industries in the cities. Indeed, kulaks were getting rich, but the cities were starving. By the spring of 1926, over 60 percent of the grain destined for sale was in the hands of only 6 percent of peasant proprietors.

The most ambitious rich peasants even tried to find ways to sell grain for a higher price on the world market, thus violating the monopoly on foreign trade exercised by the Soviet government. If they had been successful in circumventing the government's trade monopoly, there would have been even less grain available for the hungry Soviet people.

Everything came crashing down in 1928. The kulaks convinced the middle peasants to hoard grain and foodstuffs in a calculated joint effort to blackmail the government into raising prices. "The working class," Trotsky wrote, "stood face to face with the shadow of an advancing famine."

Reeling in panic at the threat posed by the kulaks, the state bureaucracy, under Stalin's leadership, broke with Bukharin. Its reaction was brutal. Agricultural products were taken from the peasants with bayonets. The kulak threat was eliminated by attempting to dissolve 25 million individual peasant holdings into 2000 collective farm units within a three-year period.

This forced march toward collectivization caused long-term damage to Soviet agriculture. Millions of peasants were killed or died from famine. And economic results were no better.

Trotsky writes that "the collective farms were set up with . . . equipment suitable . . . for small-scale farming. In these conditions an exaggeratedly swift collectivization took the character of an economic adventure." The forced collectivizations of 1929-31 were a tragic and unnecessary result of the grievously mistaken policies promoted for five years by Stalin and Bukharin. Unfortunately, these same policies serve today as the model for *perestroika*.

Situation is Explosive Today

With the country facing these problems, the prospect of a giant upheaval is not far-fetched. Gorbachev personally witnessed the rebellion of the Chinese students and workers in May 1989, proving, among other things, that the rise of Polish Solidarity in 1980 was no fluke. It was no less comforting to Gorbachev that the Chinese government has been promoting *perestroika*-type reforms for the last decade.

The architect of the Tiananmen massacre, Prime Minister Li Peng, had warned the Chinese legislature only weeks before the upheaveal that "unfair distribution of income" and other social inequalities and "chaos" had resulted from the government's market-reform policies. He suggested in a speech that a delay of up to two years in adoption of further market-oriented reforms, which were announced six months before, would be extended and that some of the reforms would even be rolled back.[15]

These changes were too little, too late in China. On the eve of the June 4 Tiananmen masssacre it was reported that inflation in many areas surged above 30 percent, corruption was widespread, growing inequality of wealth sparked further public resentment, and several regions resisted efforts by Beijing to slow state spending and economic growth.[16]

In China, the workers and peasants seem to be temporarily stunned by the shocking extent of the murderous assault in Tiananmen Square and the subsequent witchhunt against dissidents. The Chinese bureaucracy has the initiative, but at the cost of thoroughly and permanently discrediting itself.

This is a heavy price to pay for any ruling party. It means that the voices of reform will more likely organize outside the Chinese Communist Party (CCP), ultimately presenting a far bigger challenge to the CCP's monopoly of power.

But what about in the U.S.S.R.? Millions of workers and students protesting in Red Square are probably Gorbachev's biggest nightmare. Can he maintain political control while he seeks to reform the economy?

The situation in the Soviet Union is quite different from China in a number of respects. Gorbachev describes his sweeping reform efforts as a "revolution without shooting." From the moment he assumed leadership of the CPSU in 1985, he sought mass approval for his policies. He disassociated himself from the extreme political repression and forced-march economic measures of Josef Stalin's 30-year rule.

Unlike his Chinese counterparts, Gorbachev has designed a freshly painted new democratic façade for the ruling party. He says he is for "freedom of speech, press, conscience, assembly, street processions, and demonstrations." Gorbachev hopes his skillful operation will give the CPSU a new lease on life and stall significant challenges to single-party rule. There can be no doubt that maintaining the grip of CPSU is the main consideration behind the reforms.

There has not been, nor can there be, a radical transformation of Stalin's heirs. The bureaucratic machine still lives. The new faces replacing some of the worn out, tired apparatchiks will not willingly abandon their large apartments, new cars, special store privileges, and other baggage that goes along with "official" positions. Maintaining political control by the CPSU is essential to safeguarding these bureaucratic interests.

Political Bureau member and chief party ideologist Vadim Medvedev explained that, "it is crystal clear that there should be no diminution of the party's leading role. . . ."

On the question of socialist pluralism, he said, "the CPSU is open to internal discussions and also for the discussion of any issue in society by public organizations and among the non-party masses. In its relation with public organizations, the party respects their right to have an independent opinion, to uphold their own positions, and to defend their interests. Under such conditions there are no grounds for creating any alternative parties to oppose the CPSU's policy."[17]

But since the face-lift of the governing apparatus is only skin deep, it can't possibly succeed in its self-serving objective of staying in power. The wholesale rejection of leading party candidates in the March 1989 elections is only a glimpse of what the future holds.

March 1989 Elections Record Militant Mood

Gorbachev optimistically projected the March 1989 national elections as a boost to his lagging economic program. When he announced the elections at the 19th CPSU Conference in 1988, he commented that "if the political system remains immobile and unchanged, we will not cope with the tasks of *perestroika*."

Nine months later the results were in, and it's clear that he got more of a jolt than a boost. Twenty percent of the CPSU candidates were defeated. This included the top six CPSU leaders in Leningrad. These defeated apparatchiks steadfastly refused to give up their party posts, thus undermining even more the esteem of the party. Gorbachev later directly intervened to remove them.

Hundreds of other senior party functionaries lost their elections, including over 30 regional CPSU chiefs, many of whom ran unopposed. This is quite remarkable considering that 85 percent of the candidates were CPSU members and that 25 percent of them had no opposition. In these latter cases, millions of people took full advantage of the new election law, which permitted people to vote against candidates. In many cases, unopposed candidates were denied the necessary 50 percent margin of victory.

In the ethnic republics the rejection of the apparatus candidates was even more sweeping. Party leaders lost their elections in Latvia, Estonia, Lithuania, and the Ukraine—where nationalist sentiment is on the rise. A large number of pro-nationalist candidates won in these elections.

Another big winner in the elections was former Moscow CPSU chief Boris Yeltsin, who won 89 percent of the Moscow vote after being dumped from the Political Bureau for "political adventurism." According to an election poll, his popularity jumped 20 percent after the CPSU announced an investigation of his election campaign.[18]

Gorbachev often complained that people were taking the elections too seriously. "As you know, we have lately more than once encountered attempts to use democratic rights for undemocratic purposes. There are some who think that in this way any problems can be solved—from redrawing [national] boundaries to setting up opposition parties."

Most political activists understood that the elections were orchestrated from above. One person at a Moscow election rally for Boris Yeltsin which I attended in March 1989 aptly described the format: "When the government says, 'We have given you democracy, why don't you act?'—it is like saying, 'We have the orchestra, why don't you march?'"

Yet these same activists correctly used the elections as a forum for their own proposals. Debate and discussion of social, political, and cultural issues are no longer the exclusive province of the bureaucracy or its "official" organizations.

In this sense, the March elections were a thundering success for the Soviet people. Local municipal elections in the fall of 1989 were to be another opportunity for the opposition movement to sharpen its political skills—but Gorbachev postponed them until the spring of 1990.

The postponement was exclusively motivated by his concern for the party apparatus. Gorbachev made the announcement during his May 1989 inaugural address as president, presumably to emphasize his support to the party regulars, who were not in the mood for another election defeat.

At an earlier meeting of the party Central Committee in April, he had already acknowledged that local party leaders "will not participate in these [fall municipal elections] because there is a 100 percent guarantee that they will not be elected."[19]

Democracy—Gorbachev Style

Despite the democratic fanfare, the March 1989 elections for the national People's Congress were stacked from the beginning. One third of the 2250 seats in the Congress were reserved for the official "party, trade-union, cooperative, youth, women's, veterans', academic, and artistic organizations" recognized by the government. This meant that only members of these organizations, and not the general public, could vote on these nominations.

Thus, if you belonged to several groups, as many party members do, you could vote several times. Since these organizations were all blind supporters of the government for decades, it's not surprising that most found it difficult to break with the ritualistic tradition of nominating only one candidate. Only 880 candidates were nominated for their 750 seats.

The CPSU set the example by nominating 100 candidates for their 100 slots. This was a slap in the face to lower party units, which had nominated 31,500 candidates. Komsomol, the CPSU youth organization, got in the democratic spirit a bit more and nominated 102 candidates for 75 seats. And even in a few cases, like the Academy of Science, dissident candidates were able to win nomination after mobilizing the membership to overule the top echelons.

But with few exceptions, the 750 deputies in the Congress representing the "official" organizations are the bastion of support for the ruling bureaucracy. Another 750 seats in the Congress are reserved for territorial districts based on population, and 750 for the 14 non-Russian national republics.

There are two significant democratic features to the new law. First, the new election law allows complete freedom of agitation for candidates without the normal requirement of obtaining government permission for rallies or meetings. This is often violated, however.

The second democratic feature of the new law is one that allows unofficial organizations to make nominations for candidates to the national

Congress of People's Deputies. A meeting of 500 people or more in a district can make an unlimited number of nominations by majority vote.

However, after this procedure is completed, an electoral commission dominated by the party apparatus begins to screen the nominations to determine who is suitable for the final ballot. This is where the CPSU begins to assert its bureaucratic control.

The screening process works as follows: Small meetings of CPSU-dominated structures, such as labor collectives, can nominate candidates without any restrictions—unlike the district meetings, which require a minimum of 500 people. In many cases, the labor collectives and other party-controlled organizations have far fewer than 500 members. Yet, they get the same representation on the electoral commissions as the district meetings.

Thus, the electoral commissions are stacked with supporters of the apparatus. In fact, neighborhood organizations composed of pensioners, who are very dependent on the government, are also represented on the electoral commissions.

This whole procedure is designed to prevent independent candidates nominated at mass meetings from ever reaching the ballot. For example, of the four People's Front candidates nominated by mass district meetings of over 500 people in Moscow, only one made it through the electoral commission. The candidate, Sergei Stankevich, was subsequently elected as a deputy. The People's Front is the largest opposition political organization in the capital. Its program calls for socialist democracy, ecology, human rights, self-management, and an end to price increases. The mass social base of opposition forces like the Moscow People's Front explains how they were able to leap over many of the election hurdles.

Political Awakening Has Begun

The wholesale rejection of CPSU functionaries in the March 1989 national elections was the first powerful expression of the growing militancy of the population, but there have been other examples since then.

There are over 100 nationalities within the Soviet Union, many of which are now demanding an end to forced the Russification begun with Stalin's rule. Often the protests in the national republics have ended in clashes with police and troops.

There have also been several conflicts between the nationalities over historical resentments that were consciously inflamed by Stalin's policy of divide and rule. In several cases, the population balance in regions was drastically altered through massive resettlement operations initiated several decades ago.

Over time, a number of nationalities faced the prospect of being minorities in their own traditional settlements. Others felt their national identity was being erased. In one particularly grotesque example of Russian chauvinism, Stalin forced the Moldavian people to convert their traditional Latin alphabet into the Russian Cyrillic. This is not an isolated example.

In the last 40 years of systematic government-sponsored Russian settlement into Estonia, the native population has been reduced to 60 percent. Also in Estonia, Russian became the language of commerce, with Russian immigrants given priority in employment at the larger enterprises.

This grave situation contributes enormously to current national antagonisms. For example, there have been strikes of Russian workers in Estonia who feel threatened by popular demands to expand native cultural and language rights.

National conflicts are the brutal legacy of Russian chauvinism promoted during the Stalin era. These policies remain fundamentally intact despite the cessation of some of their worst features, such as the mass deportation of Tartars and other oppressed nationalities. The current heirs of Stalin still benefit from national tensions in the republics because it seems to justify their bureaucratic arguments for more central control from Moscow.

Nonetheless, nationalist aspirations for language and cultural rights, combined with economic and political demands, pose a significant challenge to bureaucratic rule and provide a tremendous impetus to the overall political struggle throughout the Soviet Union.

That is why it is so significant that the regime has been unable to organize any substantial reactionary backlash against the national minorities. On the contrary, there was mass revulsion against the April 1989 army attack against peaceful demonstrators in Tbilisi, capital city of the Georgian republic. Troops attacked the unarmed protestors with sharpened shovels and toxic gas, leaving 20 dead.

The CPSU chief in Georgia was replaced, but public outrage demanded an even more thorough investigation by the national Congress. As a result of these pressures, the government has already admitted that some form of poison gas was used. These events are signs that the fuse is getting shorter and shorter. The stage is set for even larger social explosions.

It is no secret that the CPSU lacks credibility and is incapable of putting a brake on recurring anti-government demonstrations. The party's

Moscow newspaper, *Moskovskaya Pravda*, reported that many of the most active young party candidates are defecting to join informal political organizations, where the activities are "more relevant and effective." Induction of new CPSU members fell by 20 percent in 1988.[20] Gorbachev realizes this dilemma and has moved quickly to establish authority for the Congress of People's Deputies and the Supreme Soviet.

National Congress of People's Deputies

As an alternative to the CPSU, Gorbachev wants a freshly reconstructed Congress of People's Deputies to give the stamp of approval to his anti-working class economic package. As a first step, the 1989 spring Congress passed a decree placing power into the hands of the soviets throughout the country. The supremacy of the soviets is now the law of the land, thus apparently pushing the CPSU more into the background.

The old Supreme Soviet of Stalin's time no longer exists. Few miss it. Actually, it barely functioned, seldom met, and was little noticed. It was replaced in May 1989 when the Congress of People's Deputies elected 542 deputies from among its 2250 members to serve in the new Supreme Soviet.

But, members of the new Supreme Soviet are mostly the same old faces. "There were no new names," according to Yegor Yakolev, editor of *Moscow News*, and "no political leaders who had made their debut during the latest election" were among these 542 deputies. The new Supreme Soviet actually has a higher percentage of party members than the old rubber-stamp one.

The Supreme Soviet is the major legislative body which is in session year around. It elects the president and ministers and makes the major economic and political decisions. The 2250-member Congress meets only a few times a year.

Gorbachev hopes the cleaner image of the Congress will make it easier to channel discontent out of the streets and into parliamentary chambers, where problems will be discussed in a controlled environment. A foreign correspondent for the *Washington Post* describes Gorbachev's game plan: "Ironically, the new political system won by workers' strikes will have the effect of stripping workers of much of their disproportionate power. By shifting the sources of power from communist factory organizations and unions to voters and parliaments, the reform process will probably create political coalitions that, unlike the party, can force the new austerity on workers and ignore their strikes."[21]

This otherwise accurate commentary describing the role of the new Congress contains much wishful thinking. The impending strikes and protests cannot possibly be ignored; anger reaches deep into the roots of society and engulfs the overwhelming majority of the population.

That is why Gorbachev is running fast with *glasnost*. He needs to construct a Congress with a popular track record before he begins fully implementing his economic program of *perestroika*.

But will the plan work? After only four years under Gorbachev, mass sentiment is growing tired of hearing about reforms. People want to see some changes. There already has been a noticeable change from the original skepticism, to euphoria, to enthusiasm, and back again to skepticism.

To maintain confidence among the masses for any length of time, the Congress will have to respond to the wide range of basic demands for democracy, an end to privilege, national self-determination, and more availability of consumer goods. But this is impossible. Such a development would be a threat to the Stalinist power structure.

Instead, the CPSU is trying to remain discreetly backstage, shielded from its critics, while it is in actual fact directing the whole reform movement from behind the curtain.

Bureaucrats in Control

To ensure bureaucratic control of the soviets, no other socialist parties are tolerated. The hundreds of newly formed independent political clubs are also closely monitored and harassed.

Boris Yeltsin's downfall several years ago as Moscow regional CPSU chief occurred after he allowed a wide range of independent socialist clubs to hold a national convention where numerous anti-bureaucratic resolutions were passed, including one resolution favoring a multi-party system.

Furthermore, Gorbachev's real commitment to democracy is hardly convincing. He was first elected president in 1988 by a vote of 1500 to 0 during a one-hour session of the former Supreme Soviet. This has changed somewhat in the new Congress elected in 1989. Debate and discussion is allowed, although at least one deputy couldn't restrain himself before such heresy. Watch factory director Alexander Samsonov advocated a resolution requiring mandatory unanimity.[22]

Gorbachev countered by saying that "All opinions should be expressed." But some deputies were able to dig deeper, looking beyond the superficial and shallow character of parliamentary debate to uncover the real essence of the Congress.

The curtain was lifted on the role of the CPSU. For example, Congress Deputy Igor Klyamkin had an extremely harsh evaluation of the Congress. "The time came," he wrote, "when the most perspicacious representatives of the 'apparat' realized their own survival depended on changes."

After forming the Congress of People's Deputies, Klyamkin said, the apparatchiks had the objective of ceding to "the newly elected Supreme Soviet as much responsibility and as little real power as possible. They achieved this with ease. They control both chambers of the Supreme Soviet."

"You will recall, for example," Klyamkin continued, "how Anatoly Lukyanov, then a candidate for vice president, answered the question about the division of functions between the Politburo and the Supreme Soviet. He said the Politburo would develop the policy, and the Supreme Soviet would exercise the power.

"At first sight, this is a new position which conforms to the long-established world practice of dividing the functions of political parties and the state. But in our country this can hardly be considered a solution. In this country the party having a 'leading role' constitutes one of the echelons of power, in fact the highest echelon. The party stands *over and above* the state, and as long as its position is guaranteed by the Constitution, the party 'apparat' has a monopoly on political decision-making, and therefore wields supreme power."[23]

Composition of the New Congress

Clearly, the CPSU maintains control of the Congress. First, they stack the deck by loading the Congress with representatives of "official" organizations. Then they manipulate the elections for the remaining seats by packing the electoral commissions which screen out many of the dissident candidates who were nominated by mass meetings.

But the CPSU has gone even further to ensure a compliant Congress. Unlike the original soviets—or workers' councils—in the early revolutionary history of Russia, delegates to the Congress are elected mostly from neighborhood districts. The criterion is where you live—instead of where you work.

Establishing population as the basis for representation is the standard bourgeois method, but it is the polar opposite of the original soviet form of representation, which elected delegates directly among producers at the point of production.

Working people in the cities and countryside exert their maximum power in society while they are engaged in the process of production. Working together toward completion of socially necessary tasks forges a spirit of cooperation, solidarity, and heightened class consciousness. Actual hands-on control of the major levers of production and services also provides a tremendous boost in political confidence—it's easy to sense the power at your fingertips.

Bourgeois parliaments diffuse this potential by dispersing the concentration of working people in production to neighborhoods, where the extent of social cohesion is far less. The People's Congress is modeled on this bourgeois formula for representation.

These steps are all designed to maintain bureaucratic control behind the scenes. But they have already produced some dramatic changes in the social character of the Congress that cannot be concealed. According to government figures, only 18 percent of the members of the 1989 Supreme Soviet are working class, collective farmers, or non-professional office employees—this is down from 46 percent in the former Supreme Soviet.

There are almost twice as many lower-echelon managerial personnel (chiefs of departments, work teams, laboratories, collective and state farms, etc.) represented.

Altogether, top, middle-level, and lower-level managerial personnel make up 68 percent of the newly elected Supreme Soviet. Intellectuals also doubled their representation.[24]

These figures are no accident. Contrary to *glasnost*'s carefully crafted image, government institutions are moving further away from direct influence by the majority of the population—the massive and powerful working class and farm workers.

This shift away from working-class representation contrasts sharply with the increased size of the working class. Twenty-five years ago most people lived in the countryside. Today, two-thirds of the 280 million total population live in the cities. The working class now numbers over 80 million.[25]

Perestroika reforms are admittedly not working. But neither will *glasnost* maneuvers succeed in muzzling the working class.

The objective interests of the working class, poor peasants, and farm workers can only be satisfied by the majority taking direct action. These fights will not develop within the Congress. On the contrary, the Congress will oppose these struggles.

Other forms of working-class organization, such as independent strike committees and independent unions—which are more like the factory committees and soviets of Russian revolutionary history—will appear.

The Biggest Challenge to Gorbachev's Reforms

No longer willing to defer their grievances, a national miners' strike involving over 500,000 workers was launched in July 1989. Spanning several thousands of miles, this was the largest strike wave since the revolution. It began among Siberian miners in Mezhdurechensk who had suffered 152 accidental deaths in the past year. Workers had been forced to work speed-up, overtime, and night shifts with little additional compensation.

A sit-in by 77 miners spread like wildfire throughout the coal fields. It was a fuse waiting to be lit. The strikers joined economic demands for more food, clothing, and housing, with highly developed political demands for more control over production and for stronger constitutional guarantees for individual freedom.

Workers' control of the mines, for example, almost immediately became the central demand of the strike. Some $46 million in profits were produced in the six months before the strike, but only $3.4 million was spent locally. This disparity led directly to calls for self-management of the coal industry.

Equally troublesome for the government was the formation of strike committees outside of the official trade unions. But this was inevitable, especially in the wake of the formation of Solidarnosc in Poland. Since Stalin, the official trade unions in the U.S.S.R. have functioned as partners of the bureaucratized factory management system. One local union chairman was reported to be on vacation at a rest sanatorium throughout the strike.

With virtually the whole mining sector out on a strike, the national chairman of the coal industry's official trade union tried to recoup some credibility. He told the press, "Our position is that we support the demands of the Mezhdurechensk workers."

But by that time, it was too late. The strike had already spread throughout Siberia and into the Donets Basin in the Ukraine, which has the largest deposits of coal. Demands by the Ukrainian strikers for more political autonomy paralleled those of the Siberian miners.

In an open letter to the Soviet government, the striking miners demanded "that the population in Siberia and the Far East be supplied with food in accordance with dietitian's norms, that privileges to officials be abolished and that a new national constitution be published for discussion immediately and adopted not later than Nov. 7, 1990," the anniversary of the Russian Revolution.

The entrenched, normally slow-moving bureaucracy was desperately concerned that the independent strike committees would develop an even broader political alternative to the government. Workers were pictured in the press carrying banners reading "All Power to the People's Soviets." If the strike were prolonged, the range of political demands would have undoubtedly escalated.

For that reason, rapid steps were taken to settle the strike with an infusion of money. Coal Industry Minister Mikhail I. Shchadov rushed into Mezhdurechensk carrying a pledge of $80 million in pay hikes and the promise of more local control over the mines. Other concessions included increasing the area's regular food supplies by 20 percent to 30 percent and more shipments of soap and washing powder. "It looks like within these two days more attention was paid to Mezhdurechensk's problems than within the last two decades," acknowledged *Sovetskaya Rossiya*, the CPSU Russian Federation's newspaper.

Yet, despite the concessions, workers initially rejected even the pleas of strike leaders to return to work. They insisted that Gorbachev personally explain the settlement offer. Instead, Gorbachev sent a personal appeal to end the strike on behalf of the Supreme Soviet.

Gorbachev Loses Sleep

The great lessons of this unprecedented 10-day struggle have certainly not gone unnoticed. "We've shown a strike is the only way to get what you want," said one miner. The mere thought probably keeps Gorbachev awake at night.

Gorbachev's biggest nightmare is yet to come. Even as the strikers returned to work with a bushelful of concessions in their pockets, they made clear that "they weren't going to buy us off with a bit of sausage." Strike leaders also indicated that they would not disband the strike committees. Another strike leader in the Ukraine called for "an immediate national congress of coal workers, with senior industrial managers to be excluded."[26] This could lay the basis for the formation of an independent national trade union.

The government had its predictable explanation for the strike, blaming the "inertia of local authorities." Officials were treading very carefully not to provoke the miners.

For example, *Sovetskaya Rossiya*, reported that "it is a pity that objectively [the strike] gives a negative result for the economy. But can the workers be blamed for that? People who ignored these workers' demands . . . these people are guilty." Actually, of course, the finger should be pointed at the government itself—most of all at *perestroika's* failed promises.

First Giant Steps

The Soviet working class took its first giant step in reclaiming its original revolutionary role as political leadership for the nation during the July 1989 miners' strike. This strike represented the biggest challenge to Gorbachev's economic policies so far and also showed that the workers were not yet willing to cede all their power to the revamped Congress of People's Deputies, where the CPSU still maintains control.

The most successful and powerful strike in modern Soviet history has laid the basis for a national independent union that can fight to implement the self-management perspective of the miners.

Throughout the struggle, workers' growing confidence in their own power contrasted sharply with their widening mistrust of the government. The formation of independent strike committees, one step on the road toward independent trade unions, is also only a few steps away from organizing working-class opposition parties, and, ultimately, the resurgence of genuinely representative soviets.

The example of 10 million Polish workers forming the independent trade union Solidarnosc was an unprecedented and historic event in 1980. Polish workers had an organization capable of advancing their own demands and interests against the Stalinist bureaucratic government led by the Polish United Workers Party (PUWP).

Almost 10 years later, the Soviet working class appears ready to take its first steps on this same road. There have been several attempts in the last several years. For example, the founding meeting of the Association of Socialist Trade Unions, Sotsprof, was held in Moscow in the spring of 1989. The miners' strike was still one month away, and already workers were looking for ways to form independent unions.

The meeting was attended by 30 representatives of various work collectives from 10 cities. Over 5000 workers were reportedly ready to join the new union.[27] Technically, there is no law which prevents such a development, just as there is no law which formally prohibits strikes. But, in fact, both strikes and independent unions have been outlawed since Stalin. Various legal excuses are used. These include references to constitutional provisions which state that everyone must work or laws against "social parasitism."

Despite the obstacles, there will undoubtedly be an increasing number of strikes in the years ahead. It is impossible to prevent these basic acts of self-defense by workers who are being squeezed more and more every day. But Gorbachev must prevent these strikes from getting out of control. He is attempting to provide a drawn-out legal framework for settling grievances as a substitute for militant strike action. The Supreme Soviet is now considering a law that would recognize the right to strike, but, only under certain conditions. According to sources who have seen the draft legislation, workers would have to pass over several hurdles before finally being authorized to strike. And then, it would only be the "official" trade unions who could exercise that right.

Workers confront a similar set of twisted legal maneuvers when it comes to forming independent trade unions. Whereas current law does not outlaw independent unions, in practice, it is extremely difficult if not impossible to secure proper state authorization.

Article 95 of the Fundamentals of the Law of the U.S.S.R. and Union Republics on Labor reads:

"In keeping with the Constitution of the U.S.S.R., employees are guaranteed the right to join trade unions. Trade unions act in line with their rules and are not subject to registration with state organs. State organs, enterprises, institutions, and organizations should give every assistance to the trade unions in their work."

Thus, Sotsprof has the right to recognition. Wrong. The Main Department of Internal Affairs refused to give them the all-important seal that would make them a legal organization. Lt. Col. Ivan Sedov, the official at the Main Department of Internal Affairs, said that, "It's not enough to just come here asking for a seal. Today it's them, tomorrow some anti-Soviet group. Things could go too far."

"I'm not against them creating competition for the existing trade unions," Sedov said. "But someone important should know about it and authorize it. That's the rule, and it must be observed."[28]

This bureaucratic runaround has a purpose. The regime is clearly stalling for time. Gorbachev wants to give the Supreme Soviet time to develop as the final arbiter of social disputes before granting any substantial legal rights to the working class to organize independently. The miners' strike cast a big shadow over Gorbachev's timetable. It is unlikely he will have much of a choice.

Another Course is Needed

Neither solution offered by the bureaucratic machine under Gorbachev—*perestroika* and *glasnost*—is genuine. They are economic and political maneuvers to keep the top ruling elite in power in a time of growing crisis.

But the crisis has also produced an alternative to these policies in the form of a radicalizing working class. Free trade unions, freedom of political association, the right to strike, and the right to assembly are all weapons in the hands of the majority to exert its own political will.

These weapons will be used by the next generation of fighters to carry forward the long-postponed struggle for workers' democracy and socialism.

NOTES

1. *New York Times*, June 18, 1989.
2. *Los Angeles Times*, Feb. 4, 1989.
3. *New York Times*, May 31, 1989.
4. *Business Week*, Jan. 30, 1989.
5. *Moscow News*, No. 24, 1989.
6. *New York Times*, March 19, 1989.
7. *New York Times*, Oct. 6, 1988.
8. *Moscow News*, No. 15, 1989.
9. *Moscow News*, No. 27, 1989.
10. *Sovetskaya Rossiya*, Jan. 21, 1988. Interview with L.A. Kostin, first vice chairman, U.S.S.R. State Committee on Labor and Social Questions.
11. *The Economist*, March 11, 1989.
12. *Moscow News*, No. 15, 1989.
13. *Moscow News*, No. 24, 1989.
14. *New York Times*, March 15, 1989.
15. *New York Times*, March 21, 1989.
16. *The Christian Science Monitor*, April 25, 1989.
17. *People's Daily World*, Oct. 25, 1988.
18. *New York Times*, June 9, 1989.
19. *New York Times*, May 31, 1989.
20. *New York Times*, July 12, 1989.
21. *The Washington Post*, National Weekly Edition, May 1-7, 1989.
22. *Moscow News*, No. 23, 1989.
23. *Moscow News*, No. 27, 1989.
24. *Moscow News*, No. 24, 1989.
25. *Yearbook, U.S.S.R. '87* (Moscow: Novosti Press Agency, 1987), p. 133.
26. *The New York Times*, July 21, 1989.
27. *Moscow News*, No. 25, 1989.
28. *Moscow News*, No. 25, 1989.

The Crisis of Stalinism in the post-Stalin Era

Since becoming the Soviet Union's top leader in March 1985, Mikhail Gorbachev has introduced a series of economic and political reforms aimed at pacifying the growing discontent of the Soviet working class. Gorbachev's primary concern has been to save the oppressive bureaucratic regime from a Polish Solidarnosc-type development inside the Soviet Union. In addition, he is becoming alarmed at the growing gap in the development of productive forces relative to that of imperialism.

Gorbachev and the faction of the ruling Stalinist bureaucracy he represents understand full well that bureaucratic mismanagement of the economy, chronic shortages, corruption, all-pervasive police control, censorship, and the low standard of living are generating extreme and potentially very explosive unrest among the industrial and agricultural workers, the working intelligentsia, the oppressed nationalities, and the population in general.

Gorbachev's answer to this crisis is what he calls *perestroika*—or economic restructuring. He recognizes the bankruptcy of the old-style bureaucratic caricature of the planned economy and hopes to replace it with a system that will increase the productivity of labor and the efficiency of the economy through large-scale market-oriented reforms and openings toward world capitalism.

The radical restructuring of the bureaucratic command economy also includes a degree of political openness—or *glasnost*—which seeks to attract creative scientific and technical workers and intelligentsia, who are necessary for the new growth of the productive forces. *Glasnost* is also designed to obtain the support of even broader social forces for Gorbachev's economic reform program.

Reviving the Sagging Economy

Following the examples of China and the Eastern European workers' states, the Soviet leaders are trying to revive the Soviet economy by of-

This article was originally published in June 1989 as a resolution on the Soviet Union by Socialist Action, a revolutionary socialist party in the United States in political solidarity with the Fourth International.

fering profitable openings into the Soviet economy to world capitalism. This has entailed allowing the growth of private enterprise—domestic and foreign—in the Soviet Union and the use of capitalist "incentives" such as piece-work, inflation, and unemployment to increase the productivity of the Soviet workers and farmers.

The Soviet bureaucracy is hoping that the current weakness of the world capitalist system, together with guarantees against expropriation of imperialist capital invested in the Soviet economy will encourage the imperialists to take this risk. A key guarantee being offered to imperialist capital is inherent in Gorbachev's pro-capitalist structural reforms. These changes—the introduction of market forces, decentralization of the bureaucratically planned economy, including the disbursement of control over profits among a multitude of bureaucratic entities—promise to create a more potent point of support for world capitalism within Soviet society.

This, along with recent Soviet promises to permit majority control over Soviet investments, are powerful guarantees. The imperialists are waiting only for evidence of concrete implementation, and perhaps further guarantees, before they leap. Gorbachev is gambling that his new economic policies will increase the production of consumer goods to quiet the discontent of the Soviet people before civil war erupts.

An Organ of the Bourgeoisie

An accurate description of the Soviet bureaucracy was written by Leon Trotsky in *The Death Agony of Capitalism and the Tasks of the Fourth International* exactly 50 years ago. Trotsky wrote:

"The Soviet Union emerged from the October Revolution as a workers' state. State ownership of the means of production, a necessary prerequisite to socialist development, opened up the possibility of a rapid growth of the productive forces. But the apparatus of the workers' state underwent a complete degeneration at the same time: It was transformed from a weapon of the working class into a weapon of bureaucratic violence against the working class and more and more a weapon for the sabotage of the country's economy.

"The bureaucratization of a backward and isolated workers' state and the transformation of the bureaucracy into an all-powerful privileged caste constitute the most convincing refutation—not only theoretically but this time practically—of the theory of socialism in one country.

"The U.S.S.R. thus embodies terrific contradictions. But it still remains a degenerated workers' state. Such is the social diagnosis. The political prognosis has an alternative character: Either the bureaucracy, becoming ever more the organ of the world bourgeoisie in the workers' state, will overthrow the new forms of property and plunge the country back to capitalism; or the working class will crush the bureaucracy and open the way to socialism."

Gorbachev's economic reforms clearly reveal the bureaucracy's role as the transmission belt of the world capitalist class inside the workers' state. They represent a danger to the Soviet workers and to the Soviet workers' state.

In China, similar reforms have progressed to the point where illegal private banks have been allowed to exist, where special capitalist economic zones have been established, and where corporations formed by the government in Hong Kong have been given over to the sons and daughters of the Chinese bureaucracy. From Eastern Europe to China, the workers' states have been allowing the penetration of capitalism. In so doing, they have introduced unemployment, uncontrollable inflation and the erosion of the planned economy. These societies—in which capitalist rule has been overthrown, but in which a caste of privileged bureaucrats exercises a rigid dictatorship—are incapable of efficiently operating and developing a planned economy.

Forces of Economic Regulation

The socialist form of production has at least one thing in common with capitalism: Both systems require feedback from society to regulate production; whether for use or for profit.

The capitalist motive force for production—profit—requires feedback from consumers. That is what is meant by "market forces regulating" the capitalist economy. Prices, under capitalism, are "set" by capitalists but are *determined* by socially necessary labor time. The real value of each commodity—a social substance—must pass the test of the marketplace. Commodities produced at equal costs by competing capitalists do not necessarily sell at the same price. Relatively inferior quality may result in the product of an inefficient producer commanding a price lower than its cost of production. And more efficient producers selling average quality commodities at lower prices drive their competitors out of the marketplace—and ultimately out of business.

Market forces—the sum of millions of individual acts by consumers and thousands of investment decisions by capitalists—is what capitalists really mean when they speak of freedom and democracy.

But while the market is indeed a kind of "democratic" process of "free" selection and rejection of society's product, it goes on behind the backs of society as a whole. Anarchy reigns over the capitalist market and inexorably results in critical imbalances between supply and *effective* demand. (A "demand" which has little to do with people's needs and everything to do with the purchasing power at their command.)

In a socialized economy, the productive needs of society are consciously determined. How much of each necessary product should be manufactured must be based on the available resources of labor and capital. An allocation of these productive forces is then organized for a given period of time according to a rounded plan. But here, too, social regulation is required since there is many a slip between an abstract determination of society's needs and the plan's concrete fulfillment.

The regulating mechanism *natural* to a planned economy is a function of the workers at the points of production, transportation, and distribution. This permits miscalculations—which are inevitable in any economic system—to be easily corrected when they are discovered in the very course of the process of production. And in this way corrections may be made in the very first stages, before much harm can be done.

But workers' management and control of production, and consumers self-organized to guarantee equal access by all to the best quality goods, can be operative only on the basis of a truly democratic system.

In such a democratic productive system, the plan itself may have been put together by engineers and other specialists in some office, but must be submitted for approval by the workers themselves or their elected representatives. Even approved plans, however, remain subject to persistent observation and adjustment by workers in the actual process of production.

Contrast this with the tales of mismanagement which regularly emerge from the bureaucratized workers' states. These reports, mostly coming from the bureaucracy itself, relate industrial investment decisions made by all-powerful bureaucrats who have failed to take into account some small, but indispensable, detail necessary for the project's success. More commonplace are endless reports of shoddy products placed in the marketplace by bureaucrats who "fulfill" assigned quotas without regard to quality.

But most resented by the mass of consumers in these societies are the endless hours spent waiting in line for scarce goods, while the bureaucrats shop at no-waiting stores set aside only for them.

Without democratic regulation of the production and distribution system by the producers in socialized economies, such large and small miscalculations, bureaucratic mismanagement and privilege, virtually institutionalize waste and inefficiency. Such bureaucratic mismanagement, combined with well-organized suppression of criticism, induces widespread alienation, cynicism, and indifference among the workers toward the productive process.

Workers' Control vs. Market Forces

Perestroika (the word means "restructuring") is the label Gorbachev has selected for his plan to "reform" the Soviet economic system. He has mentioned plans to open up the system to worker influence over management, including hints of "elections" of managers. Such elections, if actually implemented, will undoubtedly be Stalinist-style.

Real democracy in Soviet society is, for the bureaucracy, unthinkable. Bureaucratic privilege would crumble as swiftly as control over management personnel and decisions shifted to workers. The bureaucracy itself would be ultimately swept into the dustbin of history.

Unable to reform the Soviet economic system in a way consistent with the socialist future, the bureaucracy is compelled to look to the capitalist past for a solution. Gorbachev's "reform" program is based entirely on the introduction of capitalist market forces to cure bureaucratic economic stagnation.

Bureaucratic mismanagement of the planned economy is not to be controlled by a conscious working class free to criticize, check and correct the bureaucracy's self-serving blunders. Quite the opposite! The "reforms" tend to free the bureaucracy from the plan itself. Competition among bureaucrats for markets is the intended "corrective" mechanism.

Martin Feldstein, past chairman of the U.S. president's Council of Economic Advisers, explains his view of what Gorbachev seeks to carry out in an Aug. 26, 1987, *Wall Street Journal* piece titled "Soviet Reforms Mean Business." He describes the principal changes being developed in the Soviet economy as follows:

"*Give enterprises more discretion.* Enterprises will keep a portion of their surplus incomes instead of paying a 100 percent tax and will be allowed to use those funds to raise wages and management compensation, and expand productive capacity. . . . Enterprises are no longer to receive subsidies to cover operating losses."

Hence, "management compensation"—a euphemism for *profit*—will be promoted to enable managers to engage in capitalist-style investment—and failure in the marketplace will result in plant closures. Feldstein continues:

"*Change the character of central planning.* The proposed reforms will replace rigid planning of all production with a system of minimum production quotas set at levels that leave enterprises with substantial excess-production capacity, thereby allowing enterprises to determine their own production levels. . . .

"*Decontrol prices.* The new system will allow the wholesale prices of the discretionary product to be determined by negotiation between the enterprises that sell and those that buy. . . .

"*Create credit markets.* A major reform is now under way in which a national network of local banks will actually assess credit risks and make loans to enterprises."

And Feldstein correctly concludes:

"Any radical reform necessarily entails problems, but the Soviet goal of an economy that is half-free [sic] and half-controlled will inevitably have more severe and persistent difficulties. To succeed, the Soviet reform process may have to move far closer to Western capitalism than Mr. Gorbachev and his close advisers realize."

Imperialist Investment in the Soviet Union

Martin Feldstein's assessment reflects the wave of excitement and hopeful anticipation that has swept through the world's business leaders. The Gorbachev reforms, the world's capitalists believe, may signal more than a risky effort to make the socialized economy work better.

They are reading Gorbachev's reforms as a possible preparation to create conditions acceptable to imperialism for large-scale investment in the Soviet Union. This view is bolstered by a similar, longer-standing trend in Eastern Europe and most markedly in China.

Charles E. Hugel, president of Combustion Engineering Inc., a U.S. firm setting up a joint venture with the Soviet Ministry of Oil Refining & Petrochemical Industry, told *Business Week* (Dec. 7, 1987): "The changes being promulgated in the Soviet Union are so dramatic that a lot of companies are interested. The ones that are in early are going to get a foothold—and I think they will be successful."

Soviet leaders in the past—including Lenin—have favored such capital investment, but on terms that would not affect the integrity of the planned economy. Capitalists, on their part, have always favored investment on terms that could break down the planned economy. Even investments very profitable for Western bankers and industrialists—in the short run—are generally declined if the assistance gained for the Soviet economy—in the long run—politically outweighs imperialist profits.

To come down to fundamentals, the overriding handicap to the socialized system of production is its forced exclusion from the world market place; that is, from access to a natural world division of labor. This division of labor reflects the natural differences from country to country in each's ability to produce certain commodities most efficiently, and thus cheaply.

Those areas of the world that have naturally rich deposits of minerals and ores can produce them most cheaply. And those areas whose climates make certain agricultural products easiest to produce, also do so most cheaply. And so on.

Excluding socialized economies from access to the cheapest products available in the world marketplace compels them to waste their labor and capital in the production of certain goods, difficult for them to produce, but vital to their economy as a whole.

Making the Ruble Convertible

Perestroika economic overtures to capitalist banks and foreign markets will substantially increase pressures to accommodate to imperialism. *Time* magazine (July 27, 1987) welcomed the reforms because, "Gorbachev may represent the West's last chance, at least in this century, of better integrating the Soviet Union into the world economy. There it could come under pressure to behave like a Western country, competing for capital and markets, lowering the barriers to foreign investment, and even making its currency convertible."

In December 1988, on the eve of Soviet leader Mikhail Gorbachev's visit to New York, the Soviet government gave the green light to a series of foreign-trade reforms aimed at luring greater amounts of foreign investment to the Soviet Union.

These reforms will provide (1) wider trade rights for Soviet factories, (2) more favorable joint-venture rules for foreign capitalists, and (3) a gradual transition toward the convertibility of the ruble, the Soviet currency.

One of the main conditions demanded by the capitalists for investing in the Soviet Union is that the Soviet leadership open "free trade" doors in the state's monopoly on foreign trade. Gorbachev's December 1988 reforms do just that.

At present some 200 state factories in the Soviet Union (out of a total of around 45,000 factories) have import-export rights; that is, they can trade directly on the world market instead of going through the special state import-export houses. Beginning April 1989, all Soviet enterprises whose output is "competitive on the foreign market" will have the right to trade directly.

To attract capitalist investment, the Soviet government is also relaxing the rules governing joint ventures. These are companies with mixed Soviet and foreign capital. There are currently 130 joint ventures operating in the Soviet Union. In December 1988, the law requiring 51 percent

Soviet equity in a joint venture was scrapped. From now on, foreign investors will be able to hold controlling interests in Soviet companies. And, for the first time, foreign bosses will have the right to hire and fire Soviet workers.

A further reform that has long been demanded by the capitalists involves the Soviet ruble. Beginning in January 1990, the ruble reform will begin. The ruble will be devalued by 50 percent on various business transactions, making it cheaper for foreign capitalists to operate in the Soviet Union. Top Soviet economists have publicly stated that their goal is to have a fully convertible ruble by the year 2000. Soon after the announcement of these new measures, six of the largest U.S. corporations (Eastman Kodak, Ford Motor, RJR Nabisco, Archer-Daniels-Midland, Chevron, Johnson & Johnson, and Mercator Corp.) announced they were on the verge of signing joint-venture agreements worth billions of dollars.

Of course, the strength of any nation's currency is, in the final analysis, measured by its labor productivity. The monopoly of foreign trade was imposed by Lenin and the Bolsheviks as a protectionist measure to help shelter the young Soviet state from imperialist economic penetration. This monopoly was an explicit recognition of the fact that the relative backwardness of the Soviet economy could not be overcome without both the extension of the socialist revolution and the corresponding raising of the cultural and technical level of Soviet workers.

The vast natural resources of the Soviet state, its gold reserves, and concentrated working class were special and exceptional resources which allowed the Soviet state to survive the worldwide capitalist embargo and military intervention which followed the 1917 Russian Revolution. The "shut-in" character of the workers' state, however, with its foreign trade monopoly, was imposed by necessity. A "free-trade" policy would have ended the revolution's potential for development in a short time.

Trotsky pointed out that a stable ruble (ultimately based on gold) would best allow the Soviet state to measure its economic progress relative to the capitalist world. Bureaucratic planning implemented by an arbitrary pricing system, he argued, had to be replaced with democratic planning based on realistic determinations of value, eventually allowing the Soviet state to effectively participate in the world market with a fully convertible currency.

Trotsky posed this eventuality, of course, in the context of a monopoly on foreign trade, as well as an internationalist foreign policy. Like Lenin, he excluded the notion of "socialism in one country"—the term having been invented by Stalin to falsely convey the possibility of the Soviet economy outstripping the levels of world capitalist labor productivity without an extension of the socialist revolution to the advanced capitalist countries.

Today, *Time* magazine's wishes concerning the "better integration of the Soviet Union into the world [capitalist] economy are coming closer to realization."

Convertibility of the ruble, according to Gorbachev's overall plan for restructuring the Soviet economic system, signals the bureaucracy is preparing open "free trade" doors in the state monopoly on foreign trade, without which there cannot be a planned economy.

The free convertibility of the ruble under the conditions of uncontrolled capital penetration as is being projected would lead to the dismantling of the economic foundation of the workers' state. Allowing the uncontrolled penetration of cheaper and higher-quality commodities from other countries into the Soviet economy would undermine nationalized industry. Uncontrolled direct purchases by Soviet bureaucrats and other individuals of cheap imported goods would immediately begin to erode the socialized economy and the conquests of the October Revolution.

Soviet officials are quick to point out that the state would still have at its disposal such regulations as tariff barriers and duties on foreign products entering the Soviet Union. But these measures are by themselves ineffective in countering the devastating effects of capitalist penetration.

Tariffs and other such regulations, moreover, become subject to negotiations with imperialism when a given country decides to join the watchdog organization of international finance: the International Monetary Fund (IMF). In recent months, the Soviet bureaucracy has announced its desire to join the GATT (General Agreement on Tariffs and Trade) and the IMF. (Already Poland, Yugoslavia, and Hungary have joined the IMF.)

In an article published in the Sept. 2, 1988, issue of *Soviet Current Affairs* (No. 809), for example, a top Soviet official noted that "the entry of the Soviet Union into the International Monetary Fund (IMF) would go a long way in helping to resolve many of our internal problems."

Joining the IMF would open wide the door to submitting the Soviet planned economy to the dictates of imperialist finance capital. It could mean dismantling industries that the capitalists deem "unproductive"—such as the Gdansk shipyards in Poland—or industries oriented to meeting the internal needs of the population. It would mean austerity packages to guarantee a flow of profits to imperialist investors.

Growing Soviet Workers' Unrest

The Soviet population is becoming increasingly skeptical of Gorbachev's *perestroika* reforms.

There has been a steady and serious decline in the Gross National Product (GNP)—particularly in agricultural production—in the last two decades. And these figures have continued to drop since Gorbachev took over as general secretary of the Communist Party (CPSU).

Exiled dissident Alexander Amerisov presents an accurate picture, confirmed by numerous other reports, when he writes: "Gorbachev's policies . . . have backfired, producing misery for the Soviet people rather than benefiting them. Wages are down. Prices are up. Shortages are even greater than under Brezhnev."

Gorbachev's goal is to satisfy the minimal social needs of the population before impatient workers and peasants begin to utilize the democratic openings of *glasnost* to raise their own program. The bureaucracy is desperately trying to avoid a massive political confrontation with the working class like the one that began in Poland years earlier when similar economic austerity "reforms" were introduced.

In short, Gorbachev is in a race to keep *perestroika* ahead of *glasnost*. But, paradoxically, it is precisely the introduction of *perestroika* "market reforms" which makes a confrontation with the working class and poor farmers inevitable.

On March 2, 1989, for example, thousands of coal miners in the northern city of Vorkuta went on strike to protest the changes in production norms brought about by Gorbachev's *perestroika* reforms.

The miners demanded a six-day workweek (since 1985, they had been working with no days off), a 40 percent pay increase for the night shift, and the dismissal of many company administrators. To fight for these demands they formed an independent union and called it *Solidarnost*, a direct reference to the independent workers' movement in Poland.

On March 4, after 104 miners began a hunger strike underground, the Soviet Minister of Coal Production traveled to Vorkuta to settle the conflict. He agreed to most of the strikers' demands. He fired the mine director and agreed to the wage increases, retroactive to Jan. 1, 1989. The strikers, through their new independent union, had won.

That the first coal strike of this magnitude should take place in Vorkuta is not altogether unexpected. Vorkuta has a long tradition of anti-bureaucratic struggle. It was here that tens of thousands of supporters of Leon Trotsky and the Left Opposition were sentenced to forced labor camps by Stalin in 1936. These Trotskyists resisted valiantly, waging a 132-day hunger strike before they were mercilessly gunned down in 1938.

It was also here that a gigantic uprising of anti-Stalinist dissidents—primarily Ukrainian nationalists—took place in 1953.

In China, a 10-year period of market reforms produced the anger and frustration that exploded in the spring of 1989 with the mass mobilizations of workers and students

Austerity in Poland, demanded by the capitalist banks, gave rise to Solidarnosc. The development of Solidarnosc, although not yet victorious, confirms the prediction by Trotsky of the working class rising up against the political and economic policies of the bureaucracy. The present course by Gorbachev and others will provoke "two, three, many Solidarnoscs" throughout the Soviet bloc.

Latest Government Shake-Up

Among the most important leadership changes the CPSU made in 1989 was the elevation of Vadim A. Medvedev to a full seat on the Politburo. He was also named chairman of the party commission on ideology. Medvedev gives a good picture of where *perestroika* is going.

The economic reforms he describes are extremely far-reaching. They challenge fundamental aspects of a planned economy and seriously jeopardize a broad range of social gains made in the 1917 Russian Revolution.

"The market is an indispensable means of gearing production to fast-changing demand, and a major instrument of public control over quality and cost," Medvedev says. "Cooperative businesses and individual enterprises are effective not only in small-scale production, . . . they may also be useful in organizing . . . large-scale industry. Our previous concepts of public property . . . have proved untenable."

Nikolay Shmelyov, a leading Soviet government economist, was even more descriptive. Writing last year in the leading Soviet political and literary journal, *Novy Mir*, he said:

"We need to permit companies and organizations to sell freely, to buy freely, to buy and borrow from their reserves . . . to invest their enormous but idle resources. . . . In place of fruitless efforts at central planning . . . we should introduce contracts between supplier and consumer."

Shmelyov continued: "Only profit can measure the quantity and quality of economic activity and permit us to relate production costs. . . .

One way of reducing the current shortage of capital funds [is] for the appropriate enterprises to sell bonds to enterprises . . . and private parties as well."

None of these capitalist-like "market reforms" come cheap. They all have a price, and it's the working class and poor farmers who will pay. But most important, they extend points of support within the Soviet population for a reintroduction of capitalism and a social base of support—another guarantee—for imperialist capital.

The Cost of Reforms

There are numerous examples indicating that the reforms mean more austerity for the majority. For example, Gorbachev has strongly hinted that he no longer plans to wait two years before raising prices on consumer goods like meat and milk. He only backed away from price increases in 1987 because of strong popular resistance.

On another occasion, Gorbachev's chief economic adviser, Abel Aganbegyan, complained about the 1986 government food subsidies and said that it had become "a major problem how to get out of this mess." This messy problem for the bureaucrats—guaranteeing a basic minimum of necessities to all—is in reality one of the major social achievements of the socialist revolution despite the massive economic distortions which flow from bureaucratic administration of prices. And while Gorbachev laments over the $91 billion cost of these subsidies to the Soviet economy, it cannot be doubted for a moment that the Soviet masses well know this cost can easily be compensated by eliminating the cost of bureaucratic high-living.

Another policy shift that has caused great concern among Soviet workers is the gradual introduction of unemployment. According to Soviet economist Vladimir Kostakov, Gorbachev's economic "modernization" program could result in the loss of between 13 million and 19 million jobs within the next 10 years.

In June 1987, the government adopted a law stipulating that all laid-off workers will obtain the monthly wage of an average Soviet worker (approximately 200 rubles) for three months. Those who cannot find a job in the same branch of industry will be "recycled," that is, retrained for another job—in most cases at significantly lower pay.

Moreover, Kostakov warning that the service sector and other industrial branches might not be able to absorb the large numbers of unemployed manual workers, points to a permanent reserve army of the unemployed to keep wages down. "We are already experiencing difficulties with re-employment of the released workforce," Kostakov stated.

Indeed, Gorbachev no longer acknowledges the Soviet state's historic responsibility in assuring everyone a job. Advocates of *perestroika*, in fact, continually refer to unemployment as a "natural" part of life. And worst of all, a Soviet economy integrated on imperialist terms with the world market means that it would be dragged down along with world capitalism when the developing world crisis of capitalism slips out of control. Thus, unlike the 1930s when the entire capitalist world was wracked by economic and social crisis, while the Soviet Union made great strides forward—despite Stalinism—this time, if *perestroika* is allowed to prevail, the Soviet Union, too, will face economic, social, and political disaster.

Profit or Planned Economy?

There are other very damaging consequences for the Soviet economy as a whole if the profit motive becomes the major stimulus for production. Gorbachev was confronted with these problems during his recent visit to Siberia. He criticized many enterprises which were making a huge profit by emphasizing production of luxury items. Following the logic of the profit motive, some factory managers apparently have been shifting production away from inexpensive mass consumer items. "There are some who have simply embarked upon the anti-social road and cut down the output of cheap goods in popular demand," Gorbachev complained. "Imagine what will happen," he said, "if everyone takes this road."

That's exactly the problem. But Gorbachev should be pointing the finger at himself and at the entire privileged caste he represents. His plan for broad application of the profit motive will necessarily mean more wasteful diversions of labor and capital. A far better recourse—one which Gorbachev is incapable of proposing—would be to fully democratize the planned economy, replacing the bureaucratic administration altogether with genuine forms of soviet democracy. This would more rationally and equitably determine production for social needs. But this would require a political revolution involving the mobilization of Soviet workers against *all* wings of the bureaucracy.

Reorganizing Agriculture

Bureaucratic mismanagement of the economy is probably most acute in the countryside. Peasants neither have a sufficient quantity of equipment in good running order nor the availability of a sufficient quantity of desirable consumer products. This eliminates two key incentives for high productivity.

Why should peasants produce more if there are not enough quality goods flowing to the countryside?

Gorbachev thinks he has discovered the solution. "The substance of the current agrarian policy," he says, "is to change the relations of production on the farms." This includes promoting "contractual and lease agreements for up to 50 years."

In a dramatic speech on Oct. 13, 1988, Gorbachev called for farmers throughout the Soviet Union to be freed from the current state-run system of collective agriculture. Specifically, Gorbachev proposed that the limited experiments in leasing state lands to individual farmers should be promoted across the country. "Our idea," he said, "is that all agriculture, the entire agrarian sector, should follow this path."

Gorbachev has already encountered some problems in the countryside, just as he has in the city. Even with the colorful imagery of making "the farmer sovereign master" over the land, many farmers suspect Gorbachev's motives. *The New York Times* reports "a public jealous and resentful of the growing private entrepreneurial class."

Addressing himself to those agricultural workers who are reluctant to give up the social and economic security of the collective farms, Gorbachev remarked: "No fool is going to go to work on a lease contract as long as he can have a salary without earning it."

This statement by Gorbachev, in addition to being condescending, places the blame for low productivity in the wrong place. The major problem stifling production in the Soviet Union is not the workers—but the parasitic bureaucracy that misrules the country and who, indeed, "have a salary without earning it."

The bureaucracy, ever mindful of its privileges and of working-class opposition, today seeks to introduce market forces as a corrective for catastrophic bureaucratic mismanagement. Like socialism's capitalist critics, Gorbachev identifies low productivity with the planned economy. For a real planned economy to be effective, however, two elements are essential: the organized political intervention of the Soviet masses into actual decision-making, that is socialist democracy; and a stable money system that allows a-priori calculations to be subjected to the verification of economic life itself.

The Stalinist bureaucracy has failed to this day to stabilize the ruble so that it can serve as a reliable measure of the amount of socially necessary labor expended in the production of goods.

Two Counterposed Alternatives

There are two, opposing, objective solutions to the faltering Soviet economic system. One points forward, toward unleashing the creative power of the working class by substituting democratic control over the planned economy in the place of the existing hierarchical system of top-down bureaucratic command. The other points toward capitalist restoration.

Socialist-oriented planning requires the input of workers at every step in the process of production. Only an uninhibited democratic system of workers' control over every aspect of the economy can break the bureaucratic logjam. The workers, as producers and consumers, are the eyes and ears of the socialist system of planned production, and must be empowered to democratically elaborate, adjust, and alter the plan; oversee the standards of quality and the setting of prices; and regulate the distribution of goods.

Neither Gorbachev nor any other representative of the ruling elite can take this course. The reason is simple. Once allowed to exercise even limited control over economic and political life, the workers wouldn't stop until they wrenched complete control from the bureaucratic dictatorship.

Gorbachev knows that with the workers in the driver's seat, a process would begin that could not be stopped until social parasitism was expunged and the bureaucracy excluded from all positions of political power. Those guilty of crimes against the workers and farmers would be punished, and others, less guilty, would be re-educated and reintegrated into the economy as productive workers.

The Soviet bureaucratic caste is incapable of even risking such a profound reform. It would amount to political suicide. History has never seen such a ruling group voluntarily give up its privileges. And there is no reason to expect it now. Gorbachev, as the authentic representative of the privileged caste of bureaucrats, has opened the door to capitalist market methods for regulating the faltering Soviet economic system. As the representative of the bureaucratic caste, he has no choice but to risk the restoration of capitalism in his desperate attempt to forestall the rising wave of working-class opposition.

The Limits of *Glasnost*

It is a serious mistake to examine the democratic openings underway in the Soviet Union separate and apart from the *perestroika* reforms advanced by the Soviet bureaucracy. *Glasnost* is subordinate to *perestroika*; it is a means toward the overall objective of defending bureaucratic privilege, even if it risks the destruction of the conquests of the October Revolution.

Seeking mass approval for his economic policies, Gorbachev has dissociated himself from the extreme political repression and forced-march economic measures of Josef Stalin's 30-year rule. Gorbachev says he is for "freedom of speech, the press, conscience, assembly, street processions, and demonstrations."

In practice, of course, while there have been significant democratic openings at all levels of society—openings which the Soviet masses are seeking to open wider—Gorbachev is delivering far less than he promises. And new crackdowns are inevitable.

In early 1988 the Communist Party (CPSU) newspaper, *Pravda*, warned against the growth of unofficial political clubs and condemned advocacy of opposition political parties or independent trade unions.

"Their activities sometimes take on a clearly illegal character," the newspaper said in a front-page editorial, referring to newly organized unofficial political clubs. "Without the permission of authorities, they organize demonstrations, even disturbances. They illegally print and disseminate literature hostile to socialism."

There are numerous other examples of Gorbachev complaining that too much freedom to criticize his policies will "introduce confusion into society."

In addition, Vladimir Khlebanov, who in 1977 founded the country's first independent union, the Free Interprofessional Association of Workers (SMOT), has been in psychiatric detention since 1978. All efforts to secure his release, as well as that of the other SMOT co-founders, have been labelled acts "of imperialist destabilization."

Reshuffling the Deck

The heirs of Stalin's political machine are introducing reform measures which, unlike early Bolshevik policies, are exclusively designed to bolster their cumbersome and grossly inefficient bureaucracy.

In particular, in order to increase labor productivity, it has become absolutely necessary to relax the iron grip of the centralized bureaucracy over all aspects of the economy. But the bureaucracy is not being replaced by workers' control; it is to be placed under decentralized bureaucratic control. Gavriil Popov, a chief Gorbachev adviser, admits as much when he notes that "the tempo of change will be determined by how fast the apparatus learns new ways to lead."

Among the winners in this new deal of the cards will be factory managers and local economic administrators. The rights of the workers and the factory committees are peripheral to the real purpose of Gorbachev's reforms—which is to balance the capricious rigidity of bureaucratic centralism with anarchic market forces.

The "State Enterprise Law," enacted Jan. 1, 1988, will invest managers with control over the use of profits for reinvestment or as workers' bonuses. Even the proposed "right" to elect managers is subject to "confirmation by the superior body"—rendering it virtually meaningless.

Zhores Medvedev, a leading Soviet dissident, says that Gorbachev is not proposing "self-management . . . in any real sense. He talks about self-management in the context of the need to restrict ministerial interference" with decisions of the managers.

The Soviet government headed by Lenin and Trotsky conceived of democratically elected factory committees with control over planning and production to be the key to increased productivity, elimination of waste, and as a mechanism for correction and adjustment of inevitable miscalculations in planning.

But Gorbachev's reforms are not aimed at increasing workers' control of their enterprises. His goal is to break out of the crisis of bureaucratic management without endangering bureaucratic privilege. Most important, he has left the door open to the restoration of capitalist rights—including private ownership of the means of production. In this eventuality, bureaucratic privilege would be transformed into capitalist rights.

Democracy for Austerity's Sake?

Polish Solidarnosc developed in reaction to the same policies which Gorbachev wishes to introduce into the Soviet Union.

Gorbachev has admittedly watched Poland's experience very closely. He has observed the failure of the discredited Polish Communist Party (PUWP) to institute price hikes and other economic "reforms."

Realizing that the Soviet Communist Party (CPSU) also lacks the moral authority to successfully impose *perestroika's* austerity program, Gorbachev has turned elsewhere. He wants to complete the transformation of the "soviets" into reactionary parliament-like institutions that will be limited to giving the stamp of approval to his anti-working class economic reforms.

Gorbachev claims that he desires to limit "functions performed by the party and state bodies and [to] restor[e] in full power the soviets at all levels." This is patently false.

To achieve his purpose, he must invest the soviets with a carefully crafted "democratic" image, but one having nothing in common with the genuinely democratic soviets, which exercised both legislative and executive powers and were the foundation of the state created in October 1917.

The existing caricature of Soviet democracy can be seen in the election of Gorbachev as president of the Supreme Soviet in 1988. He was elected in a one-hour session by a vote of 1500 to 0.

The election process caps a four-year campaign to revamp the antiquated command style of government. In its wake, it has created limited openings for Soviet citizens to speak more freely and organize more openly than at any time in decades.

Not waiting for the sacrosanct formality of official recognition, thousands of political, social, and cultural clubs have recently sprung up all over the Soviet Union. *Pravda* reports that 30,000 of these informal associations exist.

Many of these are dissident working-class and socialist groups searching to discover and reclaim the original political and social goals of the 1917 Russian Revolution. The founding principle of the revolutionary state, long ago repudiated by the corrupt Stalinist apparatus, was the achievement of mass democratic working-class control over all aspects of Soviet social, economic, and political life.

In their efforts to find their way to genuine soviet democracy, workers and youth can expect no help from the current resident in the Kremlin. A closer look at today's elections in the Soviet Union makes it clear that the actual intent of the democratic reforms initiated by Gorbachev is entirely designed to keep the ruling bureaucracy in power, albeit with a cleaner image—not to establish democracy for the majority.

Gorbachev's Parliamentary System

Gorbachev's new parliamentary system, in sharp contrast to the governmental system inaugurated in October 1917, guarantees the dominance of the middle classes—and in the last analysis, the bureaucracy—over this capitalist-type democratic institution. The bureaucracy's base of support in the population narrows in proportion with its economic failures. Gorbachev's "democratization" is intended only to win allies from the middle class against the kind of threat foreshadowed by the mass worker upsurges in Poland and other Eastern European countries.

The middle classes are favored by the parliamentary electoral system, which atomizes the workers by organizing them on the basis of geographical districts rather than occupational units.

[While the Paris Commune was organized on a geographic basis, virtually the entire capitalist class had abandoned Paris. This resulted in a representative democratic system under the direct control of the workers of Paris. In every other respect, the Commune system paralleled the soviet system. The organization of the Commune and of the soviets was propelled by the same objective laws of the proletarian revolution. And the Soviet workers had been educated by Trotsky and Lenin after April 1917 to follow the example of the Paris Commune.]

The division of executive and legislative powers permits the state and Communist Party functionaries to remain free from control by any democratic institution.

The new government established by the October Revolution went beyond the parliamentary system of developed capitalism. In the parliamentary system those who control the printing presses, the radio and television systems—and other instruments for forming "public opinion"—determine the outcome of elections. This control is far more difficult to exercise when elections take place in the workplaces of the nation and in other centers where the workers, peasants, soldiers, women, and youth gather and live, where every voter is accessible to every candidate for office—and where all candidates are known to their co-workers, that is, their constituencies.

Completely free and democratic election of delegates from their workplaces to the soviet governing bodies was the single greatest conquest of the October Revolution. This *soviet* form (the word means "council") of representative democratic government, unlike the parliamentary system, combines both the legislative and executive branches in one decision-making body composed of delegates, subordinate only to the workers and farmers who elect them, and subject to immediate recall by their electors.

The true soviet system of democratic rule by the working class is directly and immediately responsive to the changing consciousness and changing needs of society. It also provides for full democratic control over state functionaries at every level.

The soviet system also works to block the degeneration of the people's representatives into a privileged caste by limiting their pay to the levels paid to workers. These qualities are what defined the new Soviet government as *the workers' and farmers' government*, in the sense of what Marx called "the dictatorship of the proletariat."

The first act of Stalin's political counterrevolution after he defeated the Left Opposition led by Leon Trotsky, was to strip the soviets of all power and transform them into decorative institutions, entirely under the control of the Stalinized Communist Party. At the same time, democracy in the Communist Party, itself, was obliterated by Stalin along with the defeat of the Bolshevik cadre that led the October Revolution. And, of course, limits on the incomes of the bureaucracy were abolished, and bureaucratic privilege institutionalized.

Gorbachev's apologists claim that he has begun a process of "revitalization of the soviet system." Nothing could be further from the truth. His "democratization" is entirely in tune with Stalin's self-proclaimed "most democratic Constitution in the world." And Gorbachev's economic reform is entirely on the order of Nikolai Bukharin's and Stalin's ill-fated policy in the 1920s of encouraging capitalist accumulation among rich peasants. This policy gave a powerful stimulus to regenerating a new class of capitalists from among this group, and from the traders that sprang up from the middle classes and the bureaucracy itself.

Calls for the Rehabilitation of Leon Trotsky

An important sign of the mass ferment in the Soviet Union is the growing number of calls for the rehabilitation of Leon Trotsky.

Sectors of the ruling bureaucracy have suggested what they call "civil rehabilitation"—as opposed to party or political rehabilitation. This would entail clearing Trotsky's name of all the phony crimes of collaborating with the fascists against the Soviet state, etc. It would entail recognizing that Trotsky had been a central leader of the Russian Revolution.

If the bureaucracy were to do this, it would be an important victory. It would demonstrate to the world that the political rationale used by Stalin and his cohorts to assassinate virtually the entire leadership of the Bolshevik Party of Lenin and Trotsky was based on lies and fabrications.

But even if the bureaucracy were to do this, the victory would be limited. If the bureaucracy is compelled to permit a limited, sanitized form of rehabilitation to Trotsky, it will be the result of tremendous mass pressure.

If forced to "rehabilitate" Trotsky, the bureaucracy must use its political monopoly to continue to falsify his role—even to the point of amalgamating his policies with those of Stalin!

Actually this campaign against Trotsky has already begun. Robert Wistrich, an expert Sovietologist, writes the following in *The Los Angeles Times* (June 30, 1988):

"The official Soviet explanation used to stress Trotsky's differences with Lenin before the revolution, his non-Bolshevik past, his 'underestimation of the peasantry,' his lack of faith in 'socialism in one country.' Today [this] is hardly relevant.

"The current line in Moscow stresses that Trotsky was no less authoritarian than Stalin, a 'superindustrializer' who believed in the militarization of labor, the regimentation of consumption, and a forced march to socialism. This Trotsky . . . is clearly an unattractive model when compared to the more moderate, gradualist Bukharin, who supported Lenin's New Economic Policy."

One of the best examples of this new fraudulent image of an authoritarian Trotsky—a Trotsky who in essence differed little from Stalin and would probably have taken the Soviet Union down the same path as Stalin—was the recent article on Trotsky in *Pravda* by General Volkogonov. This article is clearly aimed at preventing the Soviet masses from learning the truth about the co-leader of the Russian Revolution. It is a more sophisticated Stalinist attack on the program and ideas that Trotsky stood for.

We can expect more falsifications of this type in the period ahead.

Another component of the campaign against Trotsky is the charge that he was an ultraleft adventurer who was opposed to the so-called Leninist policy of peaceful coexistence among states. That was precisely what Gorbachev stated about Trotsky in his speech at the 70th anniversary celebration of the Russian Revolution.

The current mobilizations by the Soviet masses have placed the name of Leon Trotsky on the tongues of millions of people, in the Soviet Union and elsewhere. There is hardly a week in this country where you don't find a reference to Trotsky in the main bourgeois papers.

If the bureaucracy is to grant civil rehabilitation to Trotsky it must pursue its sophisticated hatchet job against him to prevent millions who are looking for an alternative from finding their way back to revolutionary Marxism, to Bolshevism, to Leninism, through its only legitimate continuator.

For our part, we must continue the struggle to clear his name as a weapon to help the Soviet masses find their way back to the heritage of the October Revolution. This renewal can only take the form of a political revolution that will sweep away the rotten bureaucracy and revive the soviets as the fundamental decision-making bodies of the state.

We must call for the publication of all the works of Leon Trotsky and their wide dissemination to the Soviet people. And we must call for the legalization of all working-class parties—particularly political parties seeking to fight for and implement the ideas of Trotsky.

The bureaucracy may finally acknowledge that Trotsky existed and that he was a revolutionary—albeit one whose ideas, like those of Stalin, were wrong. But it will never rehabilitate the soviet form of government of 1917, which would mean the destruction of bureaucratic power and caste privilege.

In order to help the Soviet masses accomplish this task, it is vital to find the appropriate way to begin rebuilding a section of the Fourth International in the Soviet Union. This must be one of the central tasks of the Fourth International in the period ahead. The basic outline of a program for the Soviet section of the Fourth International already exists in the *Transitional Program* and will be filled out in the coming period.

The National Question in the Soviet Union

One of the most explosive issues in the Soviet Union is the national question.

Lenin often referred to Czarist Russia as "prisonhouse of nations." His Bolshevik Party, immediately upon taking power, instituted into Soviet law the right to self-determination for these nations. This was an option he hoped would not be exercised, as the revolution sought to convince the oppressed nationalities that the new Soviet state would both protect their national rights and identity and at the same time advance their economic and social well-being.

Glasnost is suffering severe strains as the oppressed peoples in the Soviet Union demand the national rights granted them by the Bolshevik Revolution and retracted by the Stalinist bureaucracy. Ukranians, Latvians, Lithuanians, Estonians, Crimean Tartars, and Armenians are among those knocking on the Kremlin door demanding the right to truly sovereign homelands within the framework of the Union of Soviet Socialist Republics.

As the bureaucracy shows its incapacity to grant sovereignty, the demand for separation will grow. Under existing conditions of bureaucratic repression, the demand for independent Soviet republics by the workers and peasants of the oppressed nationalities will grow. It is an integral part of the unfolding political revolution and is entirely progressive.

Generations of Czarist and foreign oppression, followed by decades of Stalinist betrayals, have generated burning resentment among the scores of oppressed nationalities making up the Soviet Union.

There have been on-going mass demonstrations by the Armenians demanding that their republic's boundary lines be redrawn to include the Armenian enclave of Nagorno-Karabakh. These protests have been so massive that even sectors of the party intelligentsia have sided with the Armenians.

In one case, the Armenian editor of *Pravda* publicly denounced his Moscow editors for putting his name on an article condemning the Armenians; an article which he did not write and with which he disagreed. He has since been imprisoned.

The wave of regional nationalism that is rolling across the Soviet Union has also reached the shores of the Baltic. The people of Latvia, Estonia, and Lithuania are in the streets demanding the right to their language, their culture, and their national identity.

The top Soviet bureaucracy is alarmed by the intensity of national feeling in this strategic area of the Soviet Union. Demonstrations of 300,000 make the unrest obvious. Local Communist Party officials have joined the "Popular Front" mass organizations that have formed and are supporting their demands. They have done this to maintain a measure of influence as the masses react against the great Russian chauvinism of the bureaucratic dictatorship.

Gorbachev's recent proposal to remove the section from the Soviet constitution guaranteeing the right to secede played an important role in the demonstrations in 1989, particularly those in Estonia. While this section of the Soviet constitution was always ignored by Stalin, it remained a part of Soviet law as Stalin's heirs sought to maintain the illusion of continuity with the party of Lenin. Today, in the face of an upsurge of the oppressed nationalities, Gorbachev is forced to openly break with the historic Soviet position on nationalities as he strains to guarantee bureaucratic control.

The Kremlin has yielded to some demands, permitting the display of national flags, and tolerating some activities of the new national movements. Obviously the bureaucrats struggle to keep the conflict within limits they can control. For now Gorbachev hopes to maintain control without resorting to previous levels of mass repression utilized by the bureaucracy.

There is little sentiment for a return to capitalism in this explosion of nationalism. As independent states, the Latvians say, they would preserve socialized property relations, and maintain relations of fraternity and equality with the U.S.S.R. and other workers' states. Gorbachev hopes to rein in the nationalist sentiments of the Baltic people before the anti-bureaucratic revolt becomes more overtly generalized.

With the horrendous economic hardships fueling discontent in all parts of the Soviet Union the national movement on the Baltic will not be easily accommodated or repressed.

The historic position of the Trotskyist movement and of the pre-Stalin Bolshevik Party of Lenin and Trotsky is to unconditionally support the right to self-determination of the oppressed nationalities in the Soviet Union, up to and including their right, if they so demand, to secede and form independent Soviet states.

In his writings, Trotsky explained that the Bolshevik-Leninists (the

Left Opposition) would not necessarily advocate secession. While offering to grant them all their national rights, they would try to convince the nationalities to remain an autonomous homeland within the framework of the U.S.S.R.

Trotsky explained, in order to demonstrate their total commitment to the right of the national minorities to self-determination, they had to state in advance that this right included the right to secede. Without such a commitment, he said, support for self-determination would be a hollow promise.

But a new situation opened up in the period after the Moscow Trials and as World War II drew near. Writing in the U.S. Trotskyist publication *Socialist Appeal* (May 9, 1939), Trotsky explained in an article entitled "The Ukrainian Question:" "A clear and definite slogan is necessary that corresponds to the new situation. In my opinion there can be at the present time only one such slogan: A united free and independent workers' and peasants' Ukraine."

This, he explained a few months later, is a tactical question which logically flows from adherence to the principle of self-determination. Trotsky added that "the slogan of an independent Ukraine does not signify that the Ukraine will remain forever isolated but only this, that she will again determine for herself and of her own free will the question of her interrelations with other sections of the Soviet Union and her western neighbors."

New Stage of "Peaceful Coexistence"

The Gorbachev wing of the bureaucracy is also taking the traditional Stalinist policy of "peaceful coexistence" to new levels.

On the day he was elected to the politburo as chief ideologist, Vadim Medvedev put a new twist on the time-worn Stalinist policy of assisting in the defense of world capitalism in exchange for an elusive peaceful coexistence.

Medvedev actually termed the class struggle "outdated." Instead, he said, "socialism and capitalism will inevitably interact within the framework of the same human civilization." Not to be outdone by Medvedev, Foreign Secretary Eduard Shevardnadze declared that "the struggle between the two systems is no longer the decisive factor."

Gorbachev wants stability and imperialist credits to attempt to raise the Soviet economy to the level of advanced capitalism.

This utopian Stalinist policy of "peaceful coexistence" continues to have counterrevolutionary results. The Soviet bureaucracy has exerted:

• Pressure on the Sandinista government, via the use of oil shipments and credits, to make more and more concessions to the imperialists, concessions geared to undermining and ultimately reversing the Nicaraguan Revolution.

• Pressure on the African National Congress (ANC) in South Africa, via the South African Communist Party, to find a means of accommodation with the apartheid regime. This accommodation has taken the form of proposals to establish multi-chambered parliaments as in Zimbabwe. These proposals represent an open rejection of Black majority rule in South Africa.

The new "constitutional guidelines for a multiparty democracy and a mixed economy," presented by the leadership of the ANC on July 28, 1988, should be understood in this light. They represent a signal that the ANC's top leadership is willing to accommodate to the white liberal wing of the South African ruling class. The ANC is highly influenced by the pro-Moscow South African Communist Party.

The new ANC guidelines, according to *The New York Times* (July 29, 1988), "are far more specific than the Congress' 1955 blueprint for South Africa, a document known as the Freedom Charter."

The *Times* continues: "The guidelines come in response to criticism by some Western leaders and white liberals in South Africa that the Congress' platform is too vague." The guidelines announced by the ANC include "specific guarantees for the preservation of a strong private sector in the economy."

• Renewed pressure on the FMLN forces in El Salvador (via Salvadoran Communist Party leader Jorge Shafik Handal, one of the FMLN's top commanders) to form a Government of Broad Participation with sectors of the capitalist class (notably with the National Conciliation Party, PCN), with whom Handal has already publicly met, as well as Guillermo Ungo and Ruben Zamora's new party, known as the Convergencia Democrática (or Democratic Convergence).

The FMLN has been talking about taking power in 1988 or at the latest in 1989. This appears to be left rhetoric to cover up its proposal to establish a common government with sectors of the capitalist class—a popular front government.

The establishment of such a government cannot be excluded given the open political crisis of the Salvadoran bourgeoisie after the electoral victory of the ultra-right wing ARENA party in that country's recent elections. In fact, sectors of Duarte's Christian Democratic Party have begun speaking about a government of national unity that would include Guillermo Ungo and Ruben Zamora and the "responsible forces" within the armed guerrilla movement.

- Pressure on the PLO to formally break with its past positions and accept the right of the Israeli state to exist (which the PLO did at the November 1988 meeting of the Palestine National Council).

Yasir Arafat met with Gorbachev in Moscow in mid-1988 and was told explicitly that the PLO must recognize the Israeli state and its "just security concerns." The official representative from the Soviet bureaucracy present at the 19th meeting of the Palestine National Council (PNC) in November 1988, according to the Nov. 15, 1988, issue of the French daily *Le Monde* "reminded the delegates [to the PNC] of Moscow's insistence that the PLO include in its political declaration the acceptance of United Nations Resolution 242."

An article from the July 29, 1988, *San Francisco Chronicle* reports on the visit by an Israeli delegation to the Soviet Union, the first of its kind in nearly three decades:

"Until recently, Moscow demanded that Israel had to leave all Arab territories it seized in the 1967 war before it would consider a restoration of diplomatic relations. Western diplomats also say that Moscow appears to have dropped its insistence on the creation of an independent Palestinian state as part of a settlement of the Arab-Israeli conflict and may be open to other proposals. Israeli officials acknowledge a more conciliatory approach."

One such proposal includes the establishment of a Palestinian mini-state on the West Bank and its incorporation into a confederation with Jordan—essentially placing this "state" under the direct control of Jordan's King Hussein. This in essence is the Shultz plan on the Middle East previously advanced by the Reagan administration.

At a press conference on Sept. 28, 1988, the Israeli Communist Party, Raka'a, taking its lead from the Soviet bureaucracy, came out openly in support of the "confederation with Jordan plan."

Already the Hungarian and Polish Stalinist bureaucracies have renewed diplomatic relations with Israel, and Gorbachev has announced his intent to do the same. Negotiations are currently underway for the resumption of diplomatic relations between Prime Minister Yitzhak Shamir, the butcher of the Palestinian masses, and the Soviet government.

A wing of the international capitalist class has understood that an international peace conference, supported by the United States and the Soviet Union, may be the most effective way today to secure the existence of the Israeli state in the face of the deepest Palestinian uprising in history. The purpose of such a conference would be to get the PLO to agree to administer a defenseless bantustan-style mini-state on the West Bank.

Barry Goldwater, George McGovern, Philip Klutznich, former president of the World Jewish Congress and current president of B'nai B'rith, among others, recently wrote a letter to *The New York Times* (July 20, 1988) calling for a mini-state on the West Bank and for mutual recognition between Palestinians and the Israeli state.

• Pressure on the Latin American revolutionary movement to fall in line behind bourgeois-nationalist politicians and formations (often with the open support in this task of the Cuban Communist Party).

In the case of Peru, prior to Gorbachev, this resulted in the formation of the popular-frontist Izquierda Unida in 1980. In Chile, it resulted in the formation of a similar class-collaborationist current also named the Izquierda Unida in August 1987.

In Mexico, this pressure resulted in a push by the Stalinists to win support for Cuauhtémoc Cárdenas, the "progressive" capitalist candidate of the bourgeois PARM (Authentic Party of the Mexican Revolution). Cárdenas is the former ruling party (PRI) governor of the state of Michoacán. His political current is spear-headed by Porfirio Muñoz Ledo, the previous general secretary of the ruling PRI.

Although this is the same essential foreign policy Moscow has followed for over 60 years, it is an even greater counterrevolutionary threat when combined with increased reliance by the Soviet Union on the capitalist world market.

Gorbachev's foreign policy is counterrevolutionary through and through. Although it may take different forms in different sectors of the world revolution and in different countries, its overall content remains the same. It is fundamentally wrong to place a plus sign, or a neutral sign to any arena of the bureaucracy's foreign policy. The bureaucracy can play no progressive role anywhere in the world.

As of 1933, Trotsky understood that the Stalinist Bonapartist regime had become a point of support for world imperialism. He abandoned his characterization of the Stalinist regime as centrist. This analysis was the basis for the founding of the Fourth International in 1938 and continues to be the main reason today for its existence.

Political Revolution

Today, the heirs of Stalin still rule over the workers, parasitically feeding on the gains of the 1917 revolution. The bureaucratic degeneration of the first victorious socialist revolution was the result of the tragic isolation of the Soviet Union due to the delay in the world revolution—and not, in any sense, a logical result of Marxism.

The current Soviet misleaders—"reformists" and "hard-liners" alike—must be removed through a political revolution which preserves the anti-capitalist social character of the Soviet state and, at the same time, destroys the repressive Stalinist apparatus. To accomplish the task of establishing genuine socialist democracy, it will be necessary to build a new communist party inside the Soviet Union based on the revolutionary program defended by Lenin and Trotsky—a section of the Fourth International.

In September 1938, two years prior to his death, Trotsky and his supporters launched the Fourth International, a new world party committed to socialist revolution. One of Trotsky's closest associates in this effort was Leon Sedov, his youngest son. Sedov was responsible for coordinating the work of Trotsky's supporters inside the Soviet Union.

In October 1936, prior to his mysterious death in a French hospital, Sedov summed up the tasks of Soviet workers in their struggle against the ruling bureaucracy. In an article on the meaning of the Moscow Trials, he wrote:

"The Soviet proletariat can only march toward socialism by the revival and full blossoming of soviet democracy, by the legalization of all soviet parties—above all the party of revolutionary Bolshevism. But the revival of soviet democracy will only be possible through the overthrow of the parasitic bureaucracy. And the overthrow of the bureaucracy can only be accomplished by the revolutionary force of the toiling masses."

The struggle for political revolution is the struggle to defend the gains of the October revolution: nationalized property and the planned economy. It is the struggle to sweep away the rotten bureaucracy and revive the soviets as the fundamental decision-making bodies of the workers' state.

PART TWO

Leon Trotsky: The Relevance of His Ideas

Trotsky's Grandson Salutes 50 Years of Struggle

By ESTEBAN VOLKOV

Human labor is the basis of our survival and progress. It produces almost all the goods that surround us. From very old times, it has been a cherished booty.

In almost all societies known by history, there have been individuals, groups, or parasitical classes that through strength, power, or cunning have been able to get hold of other people's labor. With the advent of capitalism and the growth of population, the appropriation of human labor in the form of surplus value became more sophisticated and widely extended.

In the present world, the development of modern capitalism, with its ruthless financial imperialism, has widened the gap between the poorest, most vulnerable sectors of the world's population and smaller groups of people who are accumulating inconceivable amounts of riches and power. We also have the development of the stratified societies of bureaucratic dictatorships, where on a lesser scale, you can still find great inequalities between the working classes and the power groups.

It is a universal law that every action provokes a reaction. The unfair and heartless exploitation of huge masses of people in the dreary and unhealthy factories of the rising capitalism of the last century gave birth to the response of Marxism. Capitalism, with its more sophisticated form of slavery—without lash or chain, but with the specter of hunger for the worker and his family—was nonetheless cruel.

Marxism, the human response to this cruelty, was undertaken by Karl Marx and Frederick Engels, brilliant revolutionary thinkers with an inviolable sense of justice. They deciphered the dynamics of history, creating a rational and scientific methodology: historic materialism.

They thoroughly studied the capitalist system, discovering its laws

---

This speech was delivered by Esteban (Sieva) Volkov in San Francisco, Calif., at an Aug. 6, 1988, rally of over 300 people. The event was sponsored by Socialist Action to commemorate the 50th anniversary of the founding of the Fourth International by Leon Trotsky and a group of supporters. Volkov is Trotsky's grandson.

and its unavoidable contradictions. They dedicated their lives to the goal of erradicating forever the exploitation of the working class by parasitic minorities holding power and capital.

Karl Marx and Frederick Engels, creators of scientific socialism, or Marxist theory, provided the working class and other exploited classes with a powerful ideological weapon to struggle against all forms of exploitation, oppression, and alienation suffered in present society.

Marxism is not a crystal ball nor a magic wand. We don't have any MacGraw Hill book on "How to Perform a Successful Revolution." Marxism constitutes an essential analytical method of economic, political, and social phenomena and a basic tool for any revolutionary process.

One doesn't need to be a great strategist to understand the reason for more than a century of constant attacks and distortions against the so-called obsolete ideology of Marxism and for the persecution and extermination of many of its defenders and revolutionary leaders.

The exploited masses, according to the ruling minorities, must be kept away from dangerous ideas and loyal guides. This seems to be the simplest way to try to preserve the happy world of the fortunate minorities at the top of the social pyramid.

Enemies Within Own Ranks

Those who have damaged Marxism most, however, those who have most hampered the struggle of the oppressed, have been the disguised enemies coming from its own ranks. They have been able to confuse, mislead, and distract the oppressed working classes from their revolutionary goals. As the ship of socialism had in Karl Marx and Frederick Engels its two greatest designers and constructors, it also had two expert captains, V.I. Lenin and Leon Trotsky, to direct it across the foggy sea of conciliations, class collaboration, and reformism of the social democracy. They were able to direct the craft toward its true revolutionary road, arriving successfully at its port in October 1917 in Russia with its first triumphant revolution.

The revolutionary euphoria didn't last long. Ten years after the glorious October 1917, began the greatest betrayals and distortions of the Marxist principles of internationalism and proletarian dictatorship expressed in workers' democracy, disintegration of the oppressive state, and abolition of human exploitation.

These betrayals and distortions were brought about by the Stalinist counterrevolution, which consolidated itself during the lowering of the revolutionary tide of the exhausted and depoliticized masses in the context of the terrible scarcities and isolation of the Soviet Union. The cruel and bloody Czarist dictatorship of ancient Russia showed its repulsive face during the Stalinist dictatorship and its new court of ambitious mercenaries.

Lenin once said that the great revolutionaries, after death, are frequently transformed into harmless icons, canonized by the oppressors to cheat the oppressed masses, castrating their ideas and destroying their revolutionary cutting edge. This became especially true in his own case at the hands of the Stalinist counterrevolution. To the innumerable distortions and falsifications of the Marxist-Leninist ideals, one has to add the endless list of betrayals and crimes.

No Justification Before History

The pain and suffering brought upon hundreds of millions of Soviet citizens by the backwardness in which they lived for more than half a century and by the stupid enclosure in a schizophrenic world of total misinformation, saturated with lies and monstrous repression brought about by the bloody bureaucratic dictatorship, cannot, nor will ever have a justification before history. Nor will the authors of such aberrations obtain forgiveness.

The Stalinist counterrevolution dedicated itself to the extermination of the revolutionary vanguard of the working classes mainly inside the Soviet Union, and on a smaller scale outside its borders through its satellite parties and the executioners and bloody GPU [Stalin's secret police]. It constantly established treaties with the working-class enemies, aborting many revolutionary movements and facilitating the road for the triumph of Nazism and the Second World War.

The wounds bestowed upon the revolutionary Marxist Leninist vanguard and the exploited masses of mankind were too severe and painful. Because of this, many regimes of exploitation consolidated themselves for long periods of time, and the coming forth of a true socialism was postponed in the world. The oppressed classes and their revolutionary vanguard had many ruthless visible enemies and others hiding inside their ranks. Fortunately, though, they also had men and women of great minds and of unusual heroism and dedication who gave their whole minds, their creative energy, and even their lives for the struggle for the abolition of exploitation.

Indomitable Revolutionary

Leon Trotsky, indomitable revolutionary, great Marxist theoretician, close friend in struggle of Lenin and key element for the triumph of the Soviet Revolution, was one of these men.

His dedication, absolute loyalty to the socialist cause, mixed with his lucid and deep Marxist appreciation of his historical milieu, made him one of the first to understand in its whole severity the Stalinist bureaucratic counterrevolution; that is, the gradual transformation of the true Bolshevik Party, creator of the revolution, into a gigantic and obedient bureaucratic apparatus unconditionally under the orders of Stalin.

In 1923, Trotsky organized the Left Opposition along with other loyal and vigorous revolutionaries. He started the heroic struggle inside the party to restore the true Marxism Leninism, which was the ideological basis for the October insurrection, in defense of the exploited people. Trotsky tried to save the Russian Revolution from its total distortion and deviation, but the counterrevolution was irresistible, and the Left Opposition, which wielded a difficult and heroic struggle, was ruthlessly repressed. It went underground, and its leaders were sent to Siberia in 1928 and expelled from Russia in 1929.

While Marx studied capitalism from all its angles, disguises, and contradictions, Leon Trotsky studied the Stalinist bureaucracy exhaustively with a Marxist methodology in its morphology and physiology. Half a century later, it is almost impossible to modify his rigorous analysis and concepts of the Stalinist Bonapartism. Today Stalinism can hardly fool even a small child.

Trotsky's Most Important Task

In 1933, Trotsky considered it to be a lost cause to try to straighten the wayward roads of the Third International, which had definitively exchanged Marxism for pragmatism and opportunism and had totally abandoned and betrayed the working class.

Leon Trotsky gave himself to what he considered the most important task of his life: the creation of the Fourth International. This was a task which culminated in 1938, two years before he was assassinated.

Trotsky considered essential the creation of a new proletarian vanguard that could bravely wield the banner of Marxism Leninism and that could be prepared to take action in history. From the time of the Left Opposition, and then later in the Fourth International, Trotskyists have always been in the front lines of the fight against oppression. Trotskyism is today the main crucible of Marxist thought and action in modern history.

I am moved by a deep emotion, by the fact that at this moment we have here among us comrades, companions in struggle of Leon Trotsky and James P. Cannon, the pillars of the Trotskyist movement in the United States. They are for all of us and for the new generation a living example of courage, of full confidence in Marxism, and absolute loyalty to the working classes. I want to convey my profound admiration and respect to all of them.

The duty of the new generation of revolutionary Marxists will be to retake the banner of the fallen in order to continue with the fight for socialism and reach it. In the words of Leon Trotsky: "Life is beautiful. Let the future generations cleanse it of all evil, oppression, and violence and enjoy it to the full."

Clear Trotsky's Name!

I would like to conclude my talk by taking up another subject: the question of the rehabilitations in the Soviet Union today.

If Gorbachev's *glasnost* [openness] is to have some credibility, it is vital that there should be no forbidden areas. Leon Trotsky must be now be rid of all the avalanche of false accusations, lies, slanders, and falsifications which have been leveled at him and his ideas in the Soviet Union and the other deformed workers states for more than half a century.

Justice strictly demands that Trotsky be restored to his rightful place in the history of the Soviet Union. His works, writings, and political theses must be published, freely discussed, and objectively evaluated, as must the writings of all the others who played a role in the Russian Revolution.

The analysis and basic ideas of Marxism have in no way lost their applicability. Capitalist society has been able to generate a wealth of knowledge and scientific development. Yet it has not found—nor will it ever find—a formula to eradicate hunger, misery, and injustice from our planet. On the contrary, it has placed the human race on the edge of an infernal atomic conflagration.

The only other alternative before us is a socio-economic system in which human-kind can master its own destiny and is not just an object to be used and discarded. Real socialism or barbarism, that is our dilemma.

I would like to end up with these words: I had a very difficult childhood, very lonely and full of suffering. But today, after more than half a century, I feel like a privileged human being. I had one of the most interesting and passionate lives to have been an actor and witness to one of the most important historical moments in contemporary history.

I feel that, in a way, I am a very lucky human being to be able to see, after these 50 years of absolute darkness, a change underway in history. I feel we are starting to see some light. Today I see closer the possibility of the advent of socialism.

The Left Opposition and the U.S.S.R. Today

By PAUL SIEGEL

In the American mass media picture of the Soviet Union today 72 years of Communist dictatorship are being reversed by the innovative Gorbachev, who is introducing a limited form of democracy as a result of his realization that dictatorship doesn't work. What is true in the political sphere is also true in the economic sphere. The chronic shortages and the shoddy quality of consumer goods are proof positive that socialism is an inefficient mode of production—so the story goes.

Gorbachev, therefore, in his search for efficiency, is beginning the dismantling of the socialist structure of the Soviet Union. The system is being loosened to permit decentralization and the introduction of market reforms through which factories and industries that do not produce profits will go out of existence. Even if this causes some temporary unemployment, it will increase productivity.

Concomitant with these changes is a turn away from "Communist expansionism" in the face of internal crisis. In fact, the crisis is such that the "Russian empire" has not only ceased its aggressiveness but is itself being threatened by the upsurge of the nationalities within it. What we are witnessing, then, is the indubitable triumph of capitalism.

This mass media picture is in sharp contrast with a previous mass media picture of the Soviet Union, which was just as false and unbalanced as this one. According to the previous picture, the Soviet Union, having perfected a regime of totalitarian controls, was the one thing in the universe impervious to change. The implication was that the only way this frozen monolith could be broken up was through blows from the outside when it would come into military conflict with the so-called democracies. The media, of course, have not sought to explain how a society declared by it to be incapable of change is now seething with ideas and struggles.

Among the long-suppressed ideas that are emerging as the lid of censorship is being lifted in an attempt to let off some steam in an explosive situation are those of Trotskyism. These are the ideas that Stalin

---

Paul Siegel, Professor-Emeritus of English at Long Island University, is the co-chair of the U.S. Moscow Trials Campaign Committee.

sought to eradicate by killing those who held them. But ideas that conform to reality cannot be stamped out. When I was in the Soviet Union recently, I met aged veterans who managed to survive and continue to declare themselves Leninists and Left Oppositionists and also young people who are seeking to find their way back to the ideas of the early Bolshevik Party. The struggle of the Left Opposition against the Stalinist reaction from Bolshevism is of the utmost relevance to the situation of the Soviet Union today, and increasing access to the history of that struggle will enable a new generation to better cope with that situation. It will also help us to understand the choices the Soviet Union faces—choices which our own media only obscure—as I shall seek to show, if only sketchily.

"All Power to the Soviets"

Far from Gorbachev inaugurating greater democracy than ever existed under Communist rule, the Bolsheviks came to power, as John Reed recorded in his classic eye-witness account, after a tremendous debate in which all of Russia participated and which the Bolsheviks won, gaining the support of the workers, peasants, and soldiers. The masses of people, ordinarily the passive objects and powerless spectators of history, actively intervened in it.

The Bolshevik slogan "All power to the Soviets" was a call that the soviets—the councils democratically elected from the ranks of workers, peasants, and soldiers that had spontaneously emerged in the time of crisis—become the new form of government.

Tens of thousands of workers participated in running the state, says Marcel Liebman in his heavily documented *Leninism Under Lenin*, carrying out policies which they themselves had decided on. In the thinly populated rural areas, instead of elected representation there was direct democracy. The spirit of the times is indicated by an appeal to the population in *Pravda* of November 19, 1917: "Comrades, working people! Remember that now *you yourselves* are at the helm of state. No one will help you if you yourselves do not unite and take into *your* hands all *affairs of state*. . . . Get on with the job yourselves; begin right at the bottom, do not wait for anyone."[1]

The Bolsheviks did not seek a monopoly of power. Gorbachev has denounced the concept of a multi-party system, but Bertram D. Wolfe, a strong anti-Bolshevik who served as chief of the Ideological Advisory Staff of the Voice of America, has stated flatly, "Lenin had no idea of outlawing all other parties and creating a one-party system."[2] So too other American historians not at all sympathetic to the Bolsheviks such as Daniels and Radkey have stated that "at the time of the October insurrection the Bolsheviks as a whole had no notion of ruling the country alone."[3]

Indeed the Bolsheviks sought to enter into a coalition with other socialist parties and actually formed a coalition government with the Left Social Revolutionaries. This coalition was only broken up when the Left Social Revolutionaries, fiercely opposed to the Treaty of Brest-Litovsk, by which the Soviet government made great concessions to Germany to get a badly needed peace, engaged in an insurrection against the government of which they were members.

In the direst emergency, when the fate of the revolution hung in the balance, the Bolsheviks as temporary measures first prohibited other parties and then factions in their own party. But, says Liebman, Lenin "never depicted what he considered to be a necessity as being either a virtue or as a really lasting system."[4] Stalin made these temporary measures the norm and sanctified them as doctrine. The Bolsheviks, a party of bold thinkers and iconoclastic revolutionists, had encouraged the fullest debates within their own ranks and engaged in unending public controversy. The Communist Party under Stalin became a party of automatons accepting unthinkingly what its leadership had to say.

The Left Opposition

The struggle of the Left Opposition was to maintain what the American scholar Robert C. Tucker has called "the Bolshevik habits of criticism and opposition"[5] and to restore the previous norms of party and government. Trotsky called for the revitalization of the soviets, which had become a mere rubber stamp of the top leadership; the breaking of the grip of the ossified bureaucracy in party, government, and industry; and the legalization of all parties standing for election in the soviets. "A restoration of the right of criticism, and a genuine freedom of elections," he wrote, "are necessary conditions for the further development of the country. This assumes a revival of freedom of Soviet parties, beginning with the party of the Bolsheviks, and a resurrection of the trade unions."[6]

The American capitalist press today accepts with Gorbachev the Stalinist doctrine of the one-party system as Leninist and regards as unprecedented the current freedom of discussion, a freedom of discussion that is only a pale reflection of that in Lenin's time. So too the American press, in speaking of Gorbachev's dismantling of socialism, is accepting the Stalinist view that socialism prevails in the Soviet Union.

But the nationalization of the means of production only prepares the stage for socialism; it does not in itself constitute socialism. "It is exactly because the Soviet Union is as yet far from having attained the first stage of socialism, as a balanced system of production and distribution," wrote Trotsky, "that its development does not proceed harmoniously, but in contradictions."[7] This remains true today.

It cannot be said that this is a dismantling of socialism: it is impossible to dismantle what has not been built. This is not a frivolous semantic distinction. The great battle between Stalin and Trotsky over the possibility of building socialism in one country seemed to many in its time a battle over an abstract theory with little practical importance, but events have shown its historic significance.

"Socialism in One Country"

In denying the possibility that a backward country like Russia could attain socialism by itself, Trotsky was reaffirming what Marxists had always said: for the economic abundance that is the condition for attaining socialism, the cooperation of workers' states that have gained power in a number of advanced capitalist countries is necessary. "We have always proclaimed and repeated this elementary truth of Marxism," said Lenin in 1922, "that the victory of socialism requires the joint efforts of workers in a number of advanced countries."[8]

But the German Revolution, to which the Bolsheviks had looked hopefully, was crushed, as were the Austrian and Hungarian revolutions—and revolutionary Russia was left isolated and in want. The cumulative effects of the war, the Allied blockade, the civil war, famine, and typhus were devastating. Industrial production virtually stopped, and the working class was decimated and almost ceased to exist as a class. Many of its most conscious and self-sacrificing members were killed in the civil war; others were demoralized. Under these conditions workers' democracy receded.

A bureaucracy, many members of which were demobilized Red Army commanders accustomed to military methods and other members of which were former Czarist functionaries now working for the new state, at first served the working class but then assumed increasing independence and power. Stalin based himself on this bureaucracy, whose privileges and power he extended. Thus the failure of world revolution to come to the aid of a backward workers' state surrounded by capitalist enemies produced the development of an autocratic bureaucracy.

This bureaucracy, wedded to the theory of socialism in one country, fearful of the contagious effect of revolution abroad on its own working class, whose power it had usurped, and desirous of making deals with capitalist states at the expense of foreign workers, became counterrevolutionary through and through in foreign relations as well as at home. Far from engaging in "Communist expansionism," as the capitalist press would have it, it sought to suppress revolution.

Stalinist Betrayals

De Gaulle acknowledged gratefully in his memoirs the help he had from the French Communist leader Maurice Thorez in stabilizing postwar France on a capitalist basis.[9] The Yugoslav dissident Milovan Djilas, formerly Tito's second in command, related in his *Conversations with Stalin* how the Yugoslav revolution succeeded despite the policy and pressure of Stalin, who wished to strike an agreement with England.[10]

Jack Belden, the American correspondent who was the John Reed of the Chinese Revolution, has described how the Soviet Union signed a treaty with Chiang Kai-shek and, in conjunction with the United States, exerted pressure on the Chinese Communist Party to come to an agreement with him. It was only after Chiang, mistakenly thinking he could crush the Red Army, tore up the agreement, that the Maoist leadership, in order to defeat him, engaged, although extremely hesitant to do so, in a mobilization of the poor peasants that finally eventuated in revolution.[11]

Where the bureaucracy gave aid to national liberation movements, as in Vietnam, it did so in measured fashion in order to control and contain them. Gorbachev's policy of seeking what the capitalist press calls "regional accords"—that is, sell-outs of revolutionary struggles in South Africa, Israel, and elsewhere—is only a continuation of the bureaucracy's traditional policy.

As against this policy, the Left Opposition had an entirely different orientation. It was not under any illusion that socialism could be achieved in the Soviet Union except through world proletarian revolution, with which, world capitalism was pregnant. What was needed in the meantime was to narrow the difference between the productivity of labor in the Soviet Union and that of the advanced capitalist countries. "The more we advance," said Trotsky, "the less danger there is of possible intervention by low prices, and consequently by armies. . . . The higher we raise the standard of living of the workers and peasants, the more truly shall we hasten the proletarian revolution in Europe, the sooner will that revolution enrich us with world technique, and the more truly and genuinely will our socialist construction advance as part of European and world construction."[12]

On no account, however, he declared, should it be forgotten that in the struggle between capitalist society and a post-capitalist society far closer in many ways to capitalism than to socialism the decisive factor is revolution in the advanced capitalist countries.

This did not mean that the Soviet government should engage in foreign adventures. The capitalist press has often presented Trotsky as an advocate of the policy of exporting revolution. Trotsky was not a businessman, but he did know economics, and he knew that you cannot export if there are no buyers for your product. A good example may help to convince other countries of what can be done, but revolutions can be effected only if they grow out of peoples' most basic needs and desires. Moreover, as Trotsky put it, missionaries with bayonets are not generally welcome.[13] This is a point that Brezhnev, seeking to shore up a buffer state in Afghanistan, might well have considered.

Russian Chauvinism

Bureaucratic military action in the name of internationalism has its domestic counterpart in bureaucratic domination of the nationalities within the Soviet Union in the name of socialism. In the words of Trotsky, "[S]ince the Kremlin is the residence of the authorities, and the outlying territories are compelled to keep step with the center, bureaucratism inevitably takes the color of an autocratic Russification, leaving to the other nationalities the sole indubitable cultural right of celebrating the arbiter [that is, the central bureaucracy supposedly arbitrating between the nationalities] in their own language."[14] Gorbachev in coming forward as the arbiter between the nationalities but at the same time suppressing nationalist demonstrations in Armenia and Georgia is in line with the bureaucracy's previous policy.

Lenin in his last illness proposed to Trotsky a bloc against Stalin precisely on the issues of bureaucratism and policy toward the nationalities. He bitterly inveighed against Stalin for suppressing the rights of the Georgians and making a sham of the right of republics in the U.S.S.R. to secede inscribed in the 1918 constitution. Stalin's statement of the need for administrative centralization, he wrote, was the expression of "a quasi-imperialist attitude toward oppressed nationalities."

The "typical Russian bureaucrat" is a "Great Russian chauvinist." "The Georgian who . . . is . . . a coarse brutish bully on behalf of a Great Power . . . is offending against the interests of proletarian class solidarity. . . . Nothing hampers the growth and consolidation of such solidarity as much as does injustice toward smaller nationalities. . . . That is why it is better to show too much conciliation and softness toward national minorities, rather than too little."[15] Gorbachev, who likes to invoke Lenin, should pay close attention to these words.

"Market Socialism"

While consolidating political power in his hands, Gorbachev is reducing centralized economic planning and giving more power to factory managers but holding them accountable for maintaining factory profits. The bureaucratically centralized command structure, in which bonuses are given for fulfilling quotas imposed from above, has resulted, he has pointed out, in the production of goods of poor quality that no one wants to buy.

Fifty years before Gorbachev, however, Trotsky saw the direction in which the Soviet economy was going. In *The Revolution Betrayed* he wrote: "It is possible to build gigantic factories according to a ready-made Western pattern by bureaucratic command—to be sure at triple the normal cost. But the farther you go, the more the economy runs into the problem of quality. . . . Under a nationalized economy *quality* demands a democracy of producers and consumers. . . . Behind the question of quality stands a more complicated and grandiose problem which may be comprised in the concept of *independent, technical,* and *cultural creation.* . . . Soviet democracy . . . has become a life-and-death need of the country."[16]

The choice is not confined, as our mass media represent it, to bureaucratic centralization and market mechanisms. Instead of either the centralized system commanded by one kind of bureaucrat or the "market socialism" inviting the incursions of foreign capital commanded by another kind of bureaucrat,[17] the "democracy of producers and consumers" for which he called would be an articulated system of democratically centralized planning, with workers' self-administration in the factories and consumers' committees to guard the preservation of quality.

Market mechanisms are not new in the Soviet economy. The New Economic Policy (NEP) introduced by Lenin to cope with the disastrous situation of the Soviet Union made use of them, but Lenin characterized the NEP as a temporary forced retreat, not as the solution to all ills. Trotsky supported the NEP—in fact, he had previously proposed a policy along these lines—but he pointed to its dangers as well as its advantages.

Stalin, then in alliance with Bukharin, who is now close to being the patron saint of Gorbachev, encouraged the growth of the capitalist tendencies of the economy. Bukharin told the peasantry in a famous phrase, "Get rich!" Stalin, in response to the question asked at his instigation by a Soviet journalist if it would not be wise to deed over to each peasant for 10 years the land tilled by him, answered, "Yes, and even for 40 years."[18]

The Left Opposition, however, warned against the rise of a class of rich peasants that would hold the economy captive and proposed that the state include in its budget a considerable sum to aid poor peasants to organize cooperatives. Together with this it proposed the rapid expansion of industrial production through economic planning, not only to build a base for further development but for the production of agricultural machinery for the peasant cooperatives and for the production of consumer goods. The alliance of Stalin and Bukharin treated these proposals as the fantasies of those whom they derisively called "super-industrializers."

However, at the very time that they were mocking Trotsky's views, the differentiation of the peasantry into rich and poor was growing apace. By the spring of 1926 almost 60 percent of the grain to be sold was held by 6 percent of the peasants. The Central Committee was now forced to acknowledge that, "in connection with the further differentiation of the peasantry, the kulaks [the rich peasants—'kulak' is the Russian word for 'fist'], their economic weight growing [,] . . . have acquired the power to exert considerable influence on the entire state of the market."[19] Thus did the forces of the market threaten to swamp the nationalized economy.

The bureaucracy, which lived off this economy as its dishonest steward, reacted to this threat and adopted without acknowledgement the program of the Left Opposition but carried it out in a panic of haste in the brutal manner of Stalin and without regard for the harmonious development of the different branches of industry. In particular, the collectivization of agriculture through force rather than through patient explanation and the gradual demonstration of its advantages aroused a resistance that brought the country to the brink of disaster.

Despite, however, the great waste and tremendous human cost entailed by the methods of an autocratic bureaucracy, state planning made possible a tempo of industrialization unprecedented anywhere that has brought the Soviet Union from being a devastated backward country to being an industrial giant, albeit a malformed, limping giant. Although these bureaucratic methods, more and more in conflict with the needs of the economy, have now brought the Soviet Union into an impasse, those who denigrate state planning per se have to account for the transformation of the Soviet Union that has given it a huge, educated working class which will not indefinitely allow itself to be lorded over by its bureaucratic masters.

Political Revolution Needed

Trotsky looked to a political revolution—as distinguished from a social revolution which replaces one form of property with another—that would retain the nationalization of the means of production but would completely renovate every sphere of soviet life. "A fresh upsurge of the revolution in the U.S.S.R.," he wrote, "will undoubtedly begin under the banner of the struggle against *social inequality* and *political oppression*. Down with the privileges of the bureaucracy! . . . Greater equality of wages for all forms of labor!"[20]

It was under this banner that the Soviet miners recently struck. They expressed indignation at the special shops and other privileges of the bureaucracy and the wealth of the new entrepreneurs. "Many of the miners," says the *New York Times* reporter, "called for abolishing or sharply curtailing the freewheeling private entrepreneurs who have amassed wealth and huge resentment. . . . [P]ublic-opinion polls . . . indicate that most workers believe the state has an obligation to prevent some citizens from prospering while others fall behind."[21]

The *Transitional Program*'s statement that "the struggle for the freedom of the trade unions and the factory committees . . . will unfold in the struggle for the regeneration and development of *Soviet democracy*"[22] was given flesh-and-blood reality by the strikes, which, said the *Times* reporter, "have already given birth to a fledgling movement for independent labor organizations."[23] Its statement "*it is necessary to drive the bureaucracy and the new aristocracy out of the soviets*"[24] is similarly given reality by the miners' demands to "abolish the constitutional guarantee of the party's right to rule" and to hold "new elections to replace members of the Supreme Soviet who were chosen by official organizations like the party rather than by voters at large."[25]

As so often happens in history, inadequate reforms from on top have stimulated movement from below. The opening phase of the struggle for a political revolution has begun. Whether it will be victorious cannot, of course, be predicted. But the alternative Trotsky posed—his perception of underlying trends was so clear that he saw the process as taking less time than it actually did—is more true than ever: "either the bureaucracy, becoming ever more the organ of the world bourgeoisie in the workers' state, will overthrow the new forms of property and plunge the country back into capitalism; or the working class will crush the bureaucracy and open the way to socialism."[26]

"Socialism for the Rich"

The analysis by the American press of what is taking place in the Soviet Union, therefore, is belied by facts reported in the press itself.

Moreover, the market, which the American press has presented as the source of salvation for the Soviet Union, is very far indeed from having solved the ills of American society itself. Unemployment, to be sure, has been brought down to 5 percent, the lowest figure in 15 years, but, aside from the validity of the figure, which does not include those who in despair have given up looking for work, 5 percent unemployment not so long ago was the official definition of a depression. But the days when full employment was considered a practicable goal under capitalism are now forgotten.

Mountains of shoes are in Soviet warehouses because they are of such poor quality that no one will buy them—a great waste—but is it not an even greater waste that private owners in the so-called free enterprise system are able to discard workers, throwing them on a scrapheap as if they were broken-down machines? Or that young people are not able to obtain skills or jobs so that their capabilities rust unused?

In every large American city there are great numbers of people living in the street because they have no homes. Is it not clear that the construction industry—occupied with erecting great office buildings, luxurious homes, and expensive condominiums—does not find low-cost housing to be a profitable market? But perhaps we should take the word of the intellectual giant whose name has given us the word "Reagonomics" that people live in the street because they prefer to do so.

It would be wrong, however, to say that the state does not intervene in the working of the economy. Billions of dollars of taxpayer's money are being spent to bail out sinking savings and loans banks. There is no question here of permitting the market to take its course. This is what has been called "socialism for the rich, capitalism for the poor."

On a global scale the operation of the world market has brought to the dependent capitalist countries of Latin America, Africa, and much of Asia a colossal debt to the banks and governments of the advanced capitalist countries and a fall in real wages in the last decade ranging from 30 percent to 50 percent.

But here is a growing disparity of wealth not only between rich countries and poor countries but between rich and poor in the advanced capitalist countries as well, where there has developed what sociologists have designated "the new poverty." In the United States a recent congressional study has found that between 1979 and 1987 the poorest 20 percent of the population suffered a loss in real income of 9.8 percent while the wealthiest 20 percent of the population made a gain in real income of 15.6 percent

These disparities constitute a volatile mix bound to result in explosions. In the meantime it remains to be seen whether the U.S. economy, borne along by a dangerously inflated balloon of debt, will have a soft landing or a hard landing.

Perhaps, then, the media celebration of the triumph of capitalism is somewhat premature.

NOTES

1. Marcel Liebman, *Leninism Under Lenin* (London: Merlin Press, 1980), p. 219.
2. Bertram D. Wolfe, *Lenin and the Twentieth Century* (Stanford, Calif.: Hoover Institution, 1984), p. 179.
3. Cited by Liebman, pp. 241, 242 and n.
4. Liebman, p. 267.
5. Robert C. Tucker, "Introduction," *The Great Purge Trial*, ed. Robert C. Tucker and Stephen F. Cohen (New York: Grosset & Dunlap, 1965), p. xxix.
6. Leon Trotsky, *The Revolution Betrayed* (Garden City, N.Y.: Doubleday, Doran, 1937), p. 289.
7. Trotsky, p. 48.
8. Moshe Lewin, *Lenin's Last Struggle* (New York: Pantheon, 1968), p. 4.
9. Charles de Gaulle, *Memoires de Guerre* (Paris: Plon, 1959), vol. 3, pp. 118-19, quoted by Ernest Mandel, "Peaceful Coexistence and World Revolution," *Revolution and Class Struggle*, ed. Robin Blackburn (Atlantic Highlands, N.J.: Humanities Press, 1978), p. 296, n. 28.
10. Milovan Djilas, *Conversations with Stalin* (New York: Harcourt, Brace & World, 1962), pp. 6, 74, 82.
11. Jack Belden, *China Shakes the World* (New York: Monthly Review Press, 1970), pp. 69, 168-69.
12. Trotsky, p. 298.
13. Leon Trotsky, *In Defense of Marxism* (New York: Pioneer Publishers, 1942), p. 28.
14. Trotsky, *The Revolution Betrayed*, p. 178.
15. Isaac Deutscher, *The Prophet Unarmed* (New York: Oxford University Press, 1959), pp. 71-72, 88-91.
16. Trotsky, *The Revolution Betrayed*, p. 276.
17. Trotsky spoke of the presence in the bureaucracy of "candidates for the role of compradores [native agents of foreign capital in imperi-

al China]" who "consider, not without reason, that the new ruling layer can insure their positions of privilege only through rejection of nationalization, collectivization, and monopoly of foreign trade in the name of the assimilation of 'Western civilization,' i.e., capitalism."—*The Transitional Program for Socialist Revolution* (New York: Pathfinder Press, 1977), p. 143.
18. Trotsky, *The Revolution Betrayed*, pp. 26-27.
19. Deutscher, p. 404.
20. Trotsky, *The Transitional Program for Socialist Revolution*, p. 145.
21. *New York Times*, July 26, 1989.
22. Trotsky, *The Transitional Program for Socialist Revolution*, p. 145.
23. *New York Times*, July 25, 1989.
24. Trotsky, *The Transitional Program for Socialist Revolution*, p. 145.
25. *New York Times*, July 26 and 25, 1989.
26. Trotsky, *The Transitional Program for Socialist Revolution*, p. 142.

Prospects for Political Revolution in the U.S.S.R.

By NAT WEINSTEIN

A six-person Socialist Action delegation visited three cities in China—Hong Kong, Shanghai, and Beijing—at the end of July 1989. We had two days of discussion with our co-thinkers in Hong Kong who publish the monthly magazine *October Review* and extensive discussions with workers and students in Shanghai and Beijing.

Throughout our 10-day tour of China we were inundated with slanders hurled against students and workers by the Chinese Communist Party and government. This Stalinist bureaucratic dictatorship claims that "bad elements" had converted "honest" student protest demonstrations into a counterrevolutionary, pro-capitalist uprising. This entirely unsubstantiated charge is a rare hypocrisy, coming from the lips of representatives of a regime which has itself taken giant steps toward the restoration of capitalism in China.

After arriving in Shanghai from Hong Kong, we saw this slander hashed and rehashed in a government-issued English-language daily newspaper delivered to our hotel rooms throughout our stay. And even though we couldn't understand the language (with the exception of one member of our group) we got the same message from the visual images, depicted repeatedly on Chinese television, of manacled and cowering young people being berated by "stern" officials in military uniforms.

During our walks along the streets of Shanghai and Beijing we saw giant banners hung on many big buildings—as if it were the spontaneous action of the workers within—lauding the "defense of socialism" by the Chinese Communist Party. However, not one person among the many people we talked to, worker or student, gave the slightest credence to this lie.

We went to China with open minds, but not empty heads—we knew something of the history of the Chinese Revolution. Consequently, we went there as supporters of the conquests of the social revolution that

---

Nat Weinstein is Co-National Secretary of Socialist Action, a revolutionary socialist party in the United States in political solidarity with the Fourth International.

had abolished landlordism and capitalist anarchy in China. We went there knowing that despite the privileged bureaucracy, the living conditions of the Chinese masses had been vastly improved.

But we also went to China knowing that the upheaval was based upon mass discontent resulting from a long-simmering opposition by the masses to the ruling caste's hoggish misappropriation of a major share of the social product. We knew, too, that this discontent had been sharply aggravated by a serious decline in living standards resulting from the government's policy of reintroducing capitalist market relations.

Moreover, before leaving for China we had read all the reports on the May-June upheaval which had appeared in the American press. And we had seen the extensive coverage of these events on American television, much of it live action and interviews. As veteran political activists, we are well able to distinguish between factual reporting and the deliberate misinformation dished up by the capitalist media.

We had a few other conclusions in our heads before we left: We went to China as supporters of the struggle for genuine socialist democracy and against the privileged ruling castes, which make a mockery of socialism in the "socialist" countries. And we went as combatants in the struggle for a world socialist order. Our purpose, however, was to find out what ordinary Chinese people thought about the May-June upheaval and their perspective for the future.

We talked to railroad workers, to construction workers, to pedestrians in back-alley market-places, to workers in their neighborhoods and homes, to taxi-drivers, and to students at universities. We were careful not to leap into opening a discussion of the student-worker demonstrations since we had no idea of how closely ordinary people were being watched in China so soon after the massacre. We naturally feared that our high visibility as foreigners might endanger any Chinese expressing sympathy for protestors.

But we were quite surprised to find how ready ordinary people were to state their unqualified hatred of the ruling group—from the small-time bureaucratic chiselers to the big-time, high-living despots in the Communist Party hierarchy. There were only a few among the people we talked to who would formulate the revolutionary changes being striven for by China's masses in our terminology. But our delegation was convinced that the general opinions we heard were in substantial agreement with our own perspective—that the May-June upheaval was the opening barrage of a political, not a social revolution—that is, a revolution that would maintain the socialized property forms while instituting genuine forms of workers' democracy.

This, certainly, was in complete harmony with the grudging bourgeois news reporters' accounts, at the time, of students singing the Internationale, chanting "Workers of the World, Unite," declaring that their aim was to "make socialism better," and focusing their sharpest attacks on bureaucratic "corruption" and "privilege." Even the extensive reports on the "Goddess of Liberty," filed by bourgeois journalists, could not come up with more than the obvious allusion to the central demand of the students and workers for democracy! Not a word could be produced which could be interpreted as the "Goddess" being symbolic of a yearning for capitalism.

These opinions and judgments were fully confirmed by everything we saw and heard in China. But to fully understand the events in China, we must place it in the context of the worldwide revolt against Stalinist misrule in the degenerated and deformed workers' states. And in the second place, but no less important, China must be seen in its larger context, as an organic part of the developing crises of world capitalism.

Some Essential Background

To this day, imperialism remains unable to stabilize itself at its colonial extremities. Starting in 1917, it lost Russia. Since then, Eastern Europe, North Korea, China, Cuba, and Vietnam have also removed themselves from imperialist domination. These overturns, of course, are but the beginning; world capitalism continues to face serious crises in Latin America, Asia, and Africa. And as the overall crisis deepens, it must ultimately disrupt the equilibrium in the imperialist centers themselves.

The increasing incapability of imperialism's dependent states to maintain payments on usurious loans threatens to upset the banking system of American and world imperialism. The U.S. national treasury, which is a major guarantor of last resort, teeters on the brink of bankruptcy—into which it will tumble if no way out can be found. And the hyperinflation sweeping through one dependent country after the other is both a symptom of the developing crisis and a harbinger of things to come in the world's imperialist centers—including in the United States, the heartland of world capitalism.

There is an intimate connection between all three spheres of the coming world revolution—in the imperialist centers, in the workers' states, and in the semi-colonial countries. The delicate balance in the world economic, financial, and political structure is increasingly more difficult for capitalist rulers to maintain. Should the balance slip out of control in one of the key areas, it will tend to destabilize the entire structure—

ultimately opening up a new revolutionary period on a global scale.

The objective historic tendency taking place before our eyes is not easily perceived. In the short time we have on earth, most of us do not become aware of the connection between slow changes taking place beneath the surface of society. When these accumulating quantitative changes break out into the open, they are most often separated by years; they therefore tend to be perceived as isolated events. Even when profound confrontations dramatically erupt, such as has occurred in China, there is a tendency to see them apart from their integral place in the stream of history.

On the scale of the ordinary perception of time, the "slow" development of historic events certainly seems isolated and unconnected. But the underlying revolutionary process, which led to the liberation of nearly a fourth of the earth's population since 1917, is a continuous and uninterrupted process.

Mileposts in the Political Revolution

The first sign of the political revolution we are seeing unfold in the bureaucratized workers' states surfaced in 1953—soon after Stalin's death. There was a general strike in East Germany which shook the Stalinist bureaucracy there to its knees. At the time, I heard U.S. Secretary of State John Foster Dulles comment in the course of a television news interview on the enormous power of striking East German workers. He couldn't restrain himself from gloating over how the Communist regime was paralyzed by workers who had stopped buses and trains in their tracks, and shut factories down tight.

The East German strike was followed a year later by mass strikes in Vorkuta in the Soviet Union (which in July 1989 was one of the areas experiencing a rebellion of coal miners). And in 1956, Nikita Khrushchev, the head of world Stalinism at that time, responded to these earth-shaking warnings of coming events with his unprecedented 20th Congress speech denouncing Stalin as the murderer of almost the entire leadership of the Bolshevik Revolution.

Our newspaper at the time, *The Militant*, correctly headlined this event in two words: "Trotskyism Vindicated!" Khrushchev's admissions, however, were not judged to be evidence of self-reform, but of a deep crisis developing in the bureaucratized workers' states.

Life was quick to confirm this analysis. Later that year, Hungarian workers rose up in rebellion, took control of their factories and streets, and formed workers' councils—genuine soviets—as their democratic instrument of proletarian political power. The Stalinist regime there was sent reeling. The Hungarian army could not be relied upon to put down the uprising, and the paralyzed bureaucracy didn't dare to send them from their barracks against the people. Meanwhile, the hated police were driven from the streets by vengeful masses of revolutionary workers. The Hungarian workers' uprising could only be put down by Soviet tanks, and Khrushchev, without hesitation, ordered them to do so.

In the next 23 years we saw repeated uprisings in Czechoslovakia and Poland, and now in China and the Soviet Union itself. Up to now only the Soviet army could suppress and intimidate the elemental workers' movement against bureaucratic oppression in Eastern Europe. But the counterrevolutionary repressive role of the Soviet armed force was possible only to the extent that Soviet troops remained unaffected by the processes of revolutionary change.

That period is now near its end. We are now witnessing a mass mobilization in the Soviet Union itself. And while still in its earliest stages, it is already approaching, and in some respects surpassing, the upsurges in Poland and China. It is already clear to Gorbachev that Soviet workers-in-uniform cannot be relied upon to continue to put down strikes and revolutionary mobilizations anywhere. Each use of force—such as when troops, tanks, and a deadly version of "tear gas" were used to crush a peaceful nationalist demonstration in Tbilisi, Georgia, in April 1989, leaving men, women, and children wounded and dead—brings closer the time when Soviet troops will rebel and go over to the people.

In one sense, the Polish workers went further than any of the others in these bureaucratized workers' states so far. In 1980-81, they had organized a massive occupation of the nation's work places, which enabled them to hold the Stalinist regime at bay for a prolonged period. Still they were unable to resolve the question of power, or to even think in terms of taking physical control over the state. This was because of the presence of Soviet and other Stalinist-controlled armed forces on their borders. They correctly judged, at the time, that these foreign troops were relatively impervious to appeals for solidarity.

Chinese students and workers went further than Poles in at least that respect. They mobilized in the hundreds of thousands to employ the tactic of revolutionary fraternization with the People's Liberation Army. They instinctively knew that their army could be neutralized and won over, and that there was no foreign army close enough to intervene—much less, capable of putting down the mass mobilizations without evoking greater outrage and opposition from the awakening millions.

But workers' efforts in China to organize themselves into class institutions had only just begun. They were only at the earliest stage of organizing unions and other class institutions. They did not get much beyond spontaneous outpourings from working-class neighborhoods in support of student demonstrators. They had neither reached the point of organizing themselves in their workplaces nor had they begun to advance their own class demands.

Nevertheless, these outpourings of as many as 1 million people, the bulk of whom were workers, into Tiananmen Square and at strategic points leading into the Square, had amazing success in dissuading military convoys from attacking student demonstrators for weeks.

The revolutionary logic of proletarian struggle continues to develop throughout the "socialist" world. Now, Soviet workers are carrying consciousness to a higher level. In beginning to organize through their workplaces, they very naturally discuss and vote on their demands, and elect their committees to lead their struggle for workers' power—following the example of their Polish worker comrades. And while Chinese workers had only barely begun the process of establishing institutions of workers' democracy in the course of their mobilizations, students had gone much further. They had established such a high intensity of democratic decision-making in Tiananmen Square that one American bourgeois reporter crankily referred to it as "an obsession with democracy."

Soviet workers are especially positioned to most rapidly reach the highest levels of consciousness and self-organization. The natural course of their struggle cannot fail to evoke the memory of October 1917, when their predecessors carried the logic of proletarian revolution to its final conclusion. Almost at the very outset, coal miners have begun the Soviet workers' mass mobilizations with very advanced political demands. Miners made emphatically clear their aspiration for control over their work places and the right to determine who gets the fruits of their labor. Their demands unambiguously point toward the goal of democratic workers' management of the Soviet economy.

Today, mass consciousness is further reflected by Soviet coal miners demanding the right to decide where to put the profits from the mines. And the message they sent to the Soviet parliament set up by Gorbachev is abundantly clear. Their demand to immediately change the Soviet constitution to guarantee basic civil rights and liberties has little to do with abstract or bourgeois democracy. Above all they want their right to organize fighting class institutions to be guaranteed by law. Tomorrow, they will not fail to insist that their strike committees, factory committees, and elected workers' councils make all economic and political decisions and be responsible for carrying them out. And neither will they fail to follow this logic to its end—to drive the bureaucracy out of their positions of power. This is what is meant by "political revolution."

Gorbachev and the Soviet Bureaucracy

The *Nightline* television program on July 20, 1989, focused on the Soviet coal miners' strike. The commentators had a different analysis than ours. They suggested that the miners' revolt was the intended result of Gorbachev's new political program of *glasnost* and *perestroika* (democratization and restructuring of the economy by introducing capitalist market forces as an incentive for increasing production). They suggested that the revolt of miners is what Gorbachev was after all along; that this is what Gorbachev needed to "break the resistance" of the "conservative wing" of the bureaucracy to his economic reform program.

Anyone who really believes that Gorbachev aimed for or hoped for this working-class mobilization—or that Gorbachev or any other representative of the Soviet bureaucracy has the slightest intention to reform themselves out of existence; or that workers want, or will accept the reintroduction of unemployment or any other of the capitalist evils their grandparents and great-grandparents abolished in 1917—must also believe that the moon is made of green cheese.

Gorbachev's main preoccupation is to break the resistance of the workers to his economic reforms, which are based on austerity for the workers and the most offensive forms of capitalist incentives (such as the planned reintroduction of capitalist-style hiring and firing).

Gorbachev was convinced that this worker rebellion was coming—and soon. He feared that the threatened upsurge—which we are now witnessing—could not be put down by naked force, as in the past. He knew that the methods of bloody repression employed in the Stalin era are no longer likely to succeed in stunning the masses into submission, nor halt awakening consciousness. He knew, on the contrary, that terror could set into motion the speedy deterioration of morale in the Red Army itself—as we see it having begun to do in China. He knew that naked force must be reserved only for the last resort. And, no less importantly, it would make any attempt to find a way out of the Soviet economic crisis—which requires the toleration, if not the active support of the workers—impossible.

Moreover, history teaches that once a political regime exhausts its possibilities, as has occurred in the Stalinist bureaucratic domain, such a course of action is advisable only if it can be counted on to deal a decisive setback to the morale and will to struggle of the whole working class. Otherwise, history shows that brutal suppression may only succeed in halting a revolutionary episode at the price of smashing remaining illusions; a consequence that is invariably followed, in time, by more audacious, and more far-reaching challenges to the oppressive regime.

(In China, we were able to observe evidence of a reaction to the Tiananmen massacre from workers and students that was far from the one intended. The verdicts we heard given were unanimous. Over and over again, we were told, with this act the regime had destroyed the last remaining shred of confidence of the Chinese people.)

Gorbachev's motives for *glasnost* have nothing to do with a revolutionary reform of the Stalinist political system. His aim was to get out in front; only to appear to be leading a meaningful reform of the bureaucratic system. His policy of *glasnost* is entirely designed to put the bureaucracy in position to head off revolt before it begins. His aim is to contain the discontent within the framework of controllable forms of parliamentary democracy and bourgeois economic reforms.

Just as in capitalist America, "free elections" regularly replace one group of legislators with another; but the executive agencies of the state—the police, the army, and the ubiquitous bureaucracy which fills in all the pores of the capitalist state—remain beyond the control of the "democratically elected" legislators.

So too is this the case in the Soviet Union. The parliamentary system is inherently structured to maintain a monopoly for those in control of the executive agencies of state power, which in workers' states is proletarian only to the extent it defends workers' forms of property ownership. Gorbachev's "democracy" is purposefully constructed to separate the legislative from the executive powers of government. This is designed to permit the state to remain ruled by a caste of unremovable bureaucrats—in the military, as well as in the civil structure. And his parliamentary style democracy is being implemented in the context of his policy of weakening the anti-capitalist economic foundation of the workers' state.

In the United States, this guarantee of the dictatorship of the capitalist class is touted as "the democratic system of checks and balances." In the Soviet Union it is presented, with even less credibility, as a "revitalization of the soviets." But the parliamentary system remains in bourgeois democracies, nonetheless, a bulwark of the continued social and economic dictatorship by the capitalist class. And in the Soviet Union, it is being introduced—albeit, still a caricature of the bourgeois version—

to bolster a continued political dictatorship by the bureaucratic caste.

Gorbachev Takes a Page from Stalin

Gorbachev's democracy is entirely in the spirit of Stalin's "democratic" constitution of 1936. Leon Trotsky explained, at the time, the spuriousness of Stalin's claim. Among other things, he pointed out in *The Revolution Betrayed*:

"In the political sphere, the distinction of the new constitution from the old is its return from the Soviet system of election according to class and industrial groups, to the system of bourgeois democracy based upon the so-called 'universal, equal, and direct' vote of an atomized population. This is a matter, to put it briefly, of juridically liquidating the dictatorship of the proletariat."

Stalin, of course, followed up his "democratization" of the Soviet constitution with his launching of the infamous Moscow Trials, which purged in blood virtually the entire leadership of the October Revolution. History has so far permitted Gorbachev to go further than Stalin down the path of "democratic reform." He has succeeded, through *glasnost*, in his immediate purpose: to give false hope to the workers that real improvements in their living standards are on their way, and to provide the bureaucracy with an extended base of support among the Soviet middle class. This, he hopes, will give him time and the opportunity to patch up the faltering Soviet economy.

The middle class is most entranced by bourgeois-style democratic elections; and from their ranks comes the largest majority of professional officeholders—an indispensable byproduct of the parliamentary system and bulwark of the status quo. And similarly, the middle class is among the first to enter into the ranks of the new bourgeoisie being created by *perestroika*. The middle class also provides the bureaucrats with a more reliable base of support in the population. The bureaucracy is counting on inspiring these new allies to help pacify the workers and harmlessly channel the mass discontent that will grow along with inflation and unemployment when Gorbachev unleashes market forces.

Gorbachev has also placed himself in position to co-opt a wing of the developing independent workers' institutions—if he is unable to block them—just as Jaruzelski is doing in Poland. But he will prove unable to make it stick if he cannot successfully carry through his economic program to the point of significantly increasing the supplies of desperately needed consumer goods. Therein lies the bureaucracy's desperate gamble: If market reforms are unable to improve mass living standards in the near future, workers will increasingly mobilize to impose their own solutions—and their own methods.

But no one should misunderstand this. In rejecting the notion that Gorbachev seeks to diminish or abolish the bureaucratic dictatorship which he heads, we do not give one iota of credibility to the more Neanderthal sectors of the bureaucracy. The latter's concern is not over Gorbachev's tactics. What they fear is that these tactics won't work and will, instead, inspire greater worker opposition. The division in the bureaucracy is a product of their eroding position. It is entirely tactical and is fueled by the mounting threat of political revolution—not a division between Stalinists and anti-Stalinists, or reformers and conservatives.

Trotsky, again, showed his keen understanding of this dynamic in his prescient analysis of Stalin's constitution of 1936. He wrote in *The Revolution Betrayed*:

"In introducing the new constitution, the bureaucracy shows that it feels this danger [the beginning of an open political crisis] and is taking preventive measures. However, it has happened more than once that a bureaucratic dictatorship, seeking salvation in 'liberal' reforms, has only weakened itself. While exposing Bonapartism, the new constitution creates at the same time a semi-legal cover for the struggle against it. The rivalry of bureaucratic cliques at the elections may become the beginning of a broader political struggle. The whip against 'badly working organs of power' may be turned into a whip against Bonapartism. All indications agree that the further course of development must inevitably lead to a clash between the culturally developed forces of the people and the bureaucratic oligarchy. There is no peaceful outcome for this crisis. No devil ever yet voluntarily cut off his own claws. The Soviet bureaucracy will not give up its positions without a fight. The development leads obviously to the road of revolution."

The Source of the Economic Crisis

With remarkable insight, Leon Trotsky further foretold the current crisis of Stalinist rule in the degenerated and deformed workers' states. In 1936, again in *The Revolution Betrayed*, he pinpointed the Achilles' heel of bureaucratic mismanagement of the planned economies in the "socialist" countries:

"While the growth of industry and the bringing of agriculture into the sphere of state planning vastly complicates the tasks of leadership, bringing to the front the problem of quality, bureaucratism destroys the creative initiative and the feeling of responsibility without which there is not, and cannot be, qualitative progress. The ulcers of bureaucratism are perhaps not so obvious in the big industries, but they are devouring, together with the cooperatives, the light and food-producing industries, the collective farms, the small local industries—that is, all those branches of economy which stand nearest to the people.

"The progressive role of the Soviet bureaucracy coincides with the period devoted to introducing into the Soviet Union the most important elements of capitalist technique. The rough work of borrowing, imitating, transplanting, and grafting, was accomplished on the bases laid down by the revolution. There was, thus far, no question of any new word in the sphere of technique, science, or art. It is possible to build gigantic factories according to a ready-made Western pattern by bureaucratic command—although, to be sure, at triple the normal cost. But the farther you go, the more the economy runs into the problem of quality, which slips out of the hands of the bureaucracy like a shadow. The Soviet products are as though branded with the gray label of indifference. Under a nationalized economy, quality demands a democracy of producers and consumers, freedom of criticism and initiative—conditions incompatible with a totalitarian regime of fear, lies and flattery."

Stalinist Bonapartism and Capitalist Restoration

There are only two possible roads out of the current crisis in the Soviet Union and the other bureaucratized workers' states. One points backward toward capitalism, and the other forward to the socialist future. The latter solution, the democratic revitalization of the economic and political structure of the bureaucratized workers' states, is absolutely inconsistent with the continued existence of a privileged ruling caste.

The only road out of the current impasse, however, that is consistent with the perpetuation of privilege—is by conversion of the bureaucratic caste into a possessing class, based on the traditional rights accorded to the holders of private property in the means of production.

Trotsky explained that from its birth, the Stalinist bureaucratic dictatorship has been a regime of crisis. It performs no special role in the socialized productive system, and therefore is without roots. A rootless parasitic formation, it cannot rule with the consent of the masses. Its power is based on military-police repressive force which it exercises through its affinity and control over the privileged officer corps.

On the one hand, it bases its privileges on the conquests of the socialist revolution. But it must be on constant guard to defend these stolen privileges from the workers. Thus it must lean for support upon the neo-capitalist forces constantly being recreated in these societies, and upon world imperialism itself.

On the other hand, it must be on constant guard against the very same forces of capitalism, inside and outside the workers' state, upon which it leans for support. Those who would restore capitalism in the workers' states would much prefer to overturn the socialized property forms—and with that, sweep the bureaucracy from political power as well.

Trotsky reached into history to find a historic parallel for this phenomenon. Here he gives a brief description of the early Stalinist regime:

"Caesarism, or its bourgeois form, Bonapartism, enters the scene in those moments of history when the sharp struggle of two camps raises the state power, so to speak, above the nation, and guarantees it, in appearance, a complete independence of classes—in reality, only the freedom necessary for a defense of the privileged. The Stalin regime, rising above a politically atomized society, resting upon a police and officers' corps, and allowing of no control whatever, is obviously a variation of Bonapartism—a Bonapartism of a new type not before seen in history."

The Stalinist bureaucratic dictatorships cannot much longer maintain the status quo—balancing themselves, ever more precariously, between antagonistic class forces. Historical necessity is irrepressible. Gorbachev, Deng Xiaoping, Jaruzelski, and their ilk play no progressive role. Incapable of leading the workers' states forward, they are increasingly attracted by the pull of world imperialism. Reaching the end of their rope, they are being irresistably drawn toward a fundamental restoration of capitalist property relations.

Stalinist bureaucracies everywhere have taken the road of ever-greater dependence on imperialism. In China, and to a lesser degree in the Soviet Union, they have already given the world's capitalists a big down payment on their promises of big new openings for capitalist penetration. Imperialism, however, never in doubt over where its class interests lie, is holding back. It has given barely more than a trickle of aid, and only dangles the promise of much more to come. The imperialists are driving home the message to Gorbachev and Co. that real help will come only if more irreversible changes are made toward opening the Soviet state to capitalist penetration. Most important, they are demanding guarantees that future investments cannot be expropriated by an aroused working class.

What kind of guarantees? Imperialism requires, above all, a real economic foothold directly within the Soviet population. Parliamentary democracy is now opening the door to such a foothold in the political structure—opening a pathway to the middle classes and thus to leverage inside the Soviet political system. But imperialism requires, as well, direct economic and social agents inside the Soviet population. The right of majority control which Gorbachev and Co. are granting to foreign investors over joint ventures is another lever required by imperialism. But this concession alone is not sufficient.

What if there is a failure to honor debts or other commitments? What if a change in circumstances leads a future Soviet government to confiscate foreign investments? Legal contracts and other pieces of paper are effective only if there is a dependable social force capable and willing to back them up. At the present time such a force doesn't exist inside the Soviet Union.

The promise to permit individual managers of nationalized enterprises to negotiate contracts with each other and with foreign capital, independently of the state monopoly of foreign trade, points toward creation of such a force. It opens the possibility of transforming portions of the bureaucracy into compradores—that is, into junior partners, and thus, direct agents of imperialism. This is another guarantee being demanded by imperialism before launching any major investments into the Soviet Union.

But even that won't be enough to satisfy imperialism. They are demanding the convertibility of the ruble. A stable ruble—ideally a monetary unit that reflects real values—would be an enormous gain for the organizing of the planned economy. It would create the basis for determining the real costs of production, and thus provide an indispensable tool for steadily improving productive efficiency and far more effective planning.

But this is far from what imperialists are seeking in their demand for convertibility. What they really want is the abolition of the state monopoly of foreign trade—or at least a lowering of the barriers against the unrestricted export of cheap commodities into the Soviet economy. Such an unrestrained opening of the economy to goods produced by more advanced industrial societies with far lower costs of production would crowd domestic, nationalized, industry out of the Soviet economy.

A convertible ruble under the conditions proposed by Gorbachev would permit imperialist capital free rein inside the Soviet economy. The new class of entrepreneurs, including those who are presently a part of the ruling caste, could join the club of world imperialism's junior partners who keep at least a reserve portion of their wealth in imperialist bank accounts and invest it in foreign, as well as domestic, enterprises. This little detail, too, will help cement the bond between this neo-capitalist layer and the world's intransigent opponents of socialism. Imperialism, thus, would be well on the road to establishing a dependable social agency for defending the sanctity of private property inside the Soviet Union.

The state sector would gradually come under the domination of forms of private ownership: first, perhaps, Chinese-style cooperatives with shareholding by the enterprise's employees and management, and later by the sale of shares outside the enterprise. Eventually, the Soviet economy would become entirely subjugated by imperialist capital.

A good example of what the imperialists have in mind is revealed in a guest column by Paul Craig Roberts in the July 20, 1989, *Christian Science Monitor*. Roberts had been invited to appear before "Mr. Gorbachev's reformers" at the Soviet Academy of Sciences. Asked to present his case for the restoration of capitalism, he argued that it is the only solution for the "collapsing" Soviet economy. He writes:

"Nothing can be done until private property rights are established. Peasants will have to be given the land and workers and managers will have to become the owners of the factories. Once property rights are assigned, prices can reflect true values, and the Soviet economy can begin its recovery from 70 years of socialism.

"All of this made sense to my sophisticated Moscow audience. Still the question arose, 'What do we do with the Communist Party?' 'Give them a disproportionate share of the new ownership rights,' I said, 'and make them the idle rich.'

"Soviet reformers saw this as a common-sense proposition. Historically, ruling classes have had to be accommodated or overthrown. Golden parachutes for Communist Party members is an inexpensive way of obtaining an efficient private economy."

Of course, Gorbachev will not lightly launch such a definitive course toward capitalist restoration. He knows that the Soviet workers will have a thing or two to say about it. His initial economic cure already requires the workers to swallow some bitter medicine. According to the bureaucracy, that merely would be a "temporary" decline in living standards. But already, the miners have not only rejected further cuts in living standards, they have forced real concessions from Gorbachev.

And how will the bureaucracy refuse similar demands from the rest of the Soviet working class? Gorbachev, unable to put his "restructuring" of the Soviet economy into effect so far, has been forced to retreat before he could begin to force his capitalist medicine down workers' throats.

Furthermore, the bureaucracy as a whole is not ready to leap into the unchartered and perilous waters of capitalist restoration. But their choices are increasingly being restricted by the proletarian Scylla pressing in on one flank, and the imperialist Charybdis on the other. But these choices are not symmetrical. As the *Monitor* columnist suggests, the latter option has the advantage of golden parachutes for the ruling bureaucratic caste, while the former denies them such a soft landing. In the long run, it is an absolute certainty, the bureaucracy in its overwhelming majority will opt for the golden parachute, not socialist democracy. A bitter struggle between workers on one side and bureaucrats and bosses on the other is inevitable.

Revolutionary Leadership Is Indispensable

To win this unfolding struggle, the workers will have to create a revolutionary party to lead them through the complex tactical problems all revolutionary classes face. To win in the struggle for political power, the world's workers must build a leadership that understands history and its lessons.

As can be seen in Poland, this consciousness is developing; the differentiation between the reformists in Solidarity and the future cadres of the revolutionary party has already begun to take place.

The basic program for such parties everywhere—including in the so-called socialist countries—already exists. It goes by the name of *The Transitional Program for Socialist Revolution*. This document is, of course, buttressed by the wealth of theoretical and programmatic conquests of the revolutionary Marxist movement, which is continuously and consistently being updated as new events occur.

This is neither pretentiousness nor sectarian self-delusion. The test of any scientific thesis is its ability to predict. The *Transitional Program*—the basic programmatic foundation of the Fourth International (F.I.), written by Leon Trotsky and adopted by the founding convention of the F.I. in 1938—has already passed this test.

This document, together with Trotsky's fundamental analysis of the Soviet degeneration—*The Revolution Betrayed*—which outlines the program for political revolution in the Soviet Union, and social revolution in the capitalist world should be read by everyone who wants to understand the current crisis of Stalinism and to find a way forward in the United States and other capitalist countries. Let me cite only the most recent confirmation of the power of revolutionary Marxist political analysis contained in the *Transitional Program for Socialist Revolution*. In 1938, the author of this basic document predicted:

"A fresh upsurge of the revolution in the U.S.S.R. will begin under the banner of the struggle against social inequality and political oppression. . . .

"The struggle for the freedom of the trade unions and the factory committees, for the right of assembly and freedom of the press, will unfold in the struggle for the regeneration and development of Soviet democracy.

"The bureaucracy replaced the soviets as class organs with the fiction of universal electoral rights—in the style of Hitler-Goebels. It is necessary to return to the soviets not only their free democratic form but also their class content. As once the bourgeoisie and kulaks [rich peasants] were not permitted to enter the soviets, so now it is necessary to drive the bureaucracy and the new aristocracy out of the soviets!"

The struggle has begun in Poland, China, and the Soviet Union, as we have seen, exactly as was then projected. Events pile on events bringing the programmatic view of the future to life. On July 21, 1989, *The New York Times* reported on a strike leader in Rostov-on-Don who declared he speaks for all the coal field workers in that southern Russian mining area. He called for an immediate national congress of coal workers with senior industrial managers to be excluded.

Every such event confirms the viability of our program. It is as if it were written just yesterday.

Revolutionary Internationalism

I will conclude by discussing the question of the perspective of world revolution today. The organic connection between the revolutionary workers' struggle in each country to every other is obvious. The world economy is dominated by the advanced capitalist countries. They exclude the workers' states from free access to the world division of labor. This places an intolerable extra burden on these countries, which had been among the most underdeveloped in the world before overturning capitalism. They have all been struggling merely to catch up with the advanced capitalist countries and still have a long way to go. They cannot succeed in catching up without the help of one or more of the advanced industrial countries—not to mention surpassing them and entering the era of socialism.

Lenin and Trotsky and their Bolshevik Party never for an instant failed to recognize this fundamental materialist conception of the road to socialism. The Bolsheviks, from the outset, called for the formation of the Third or Communist International (Comintern) to extend the socialist revolution beyond Soviet borders and ultimately to the whole world. This, it was explained, was the only road to socialism anywhere.

The Comintern, the world party of socialist revolution, was founded in March 1919. Its goal was unequivocal: to defend the first workers' state, which was seen as the advanced outpost of the world revolution, and to carry the banner of socialist revolution wherever objective conditions opened up the possibility of establishing workers' republics.

The leaders of the Third International—especially Lenin, Trotsky, and their Bolshevik Party—focused their attention on Germany, which was in revolutionary turmoil. Lenin and Trotsky never wavered from this fundamental outlook and the course of action it dictated. It was Stalin, and the bureaucracy—whose caste interests he came to incarnate—who abandoned the revolutionary perspective of extending the revolution to the advanced countries and toward a world socialist society. Stalin's slogan, "Socialism in One Country!" became the euphemism for worldwide class collaboration, counterrevolution, and in reality, "Socialism in No Country!"

Revolutionary opportunities were at first missed, and by 1927—with Stalin's counterrevolutionary policy definitively put into effect in China—betrayed in one country after the other. This opened the door to World War II and further betrayals. Ultimately this allowed world capitalism to become restabilized—at least in its imperialist strongholds—for an unprecedented four decades.

The consequent decline in revolutionary mobilizations in the centers of imperialist power in great part explains why revolutionary movements, which have had much greater successes at the extremities of imperialist power, have tended to keep a blind eye toward the perspective of world revolution. Workers' revolution in these key areas of world capitalism seems far fetched to revolutionary-minded masses in these countries. This should not be surprising given the current context of relatively low levels of class struggle inside the advanced capitalist countries. This same factor also explains the weakness of the Fourth International, whose entire programmatic outlook is organically founded on the perspective of world revolution.

We are reaching the end of that period. The forces of history, blocked for so long by subjective factors—the absence of a mass revolutionary leadership—relentlessly builds up behind these barriers. Evidence accumulates that the historical logjam is about to break open. And with the collapse of world capitalist equilibrium will also come the revival of the perspective of world revolution.

When that time comes, the program for world revolution, summed up in outline form in the *Transitional Program*, is certain to gain millions of new adherents. And the working class in the strongholds of world capitalism is destined, once again, to take the center stage of history.

PART THREE

Trotskyists Return to the Soviet Union

A Trotskyist in Moscow

By PIERRE BROUE

I became a Trotskyist in 1944 at the age of 18. France was under Nazi occupation. From the day I joined the Trotskyist movement I became a Communist and an Internationalist. I have remained a Trotskyist ever since.

I have always been fascinated by the history of the Soviet Union, particularly the struggle of the Left Opposition, led by Leon Trotsky, against the degeneration of the Bolshevik Party and Soviet workers' state. As an historian I became a specialist of 20th century revolutions and published several books on Germany, Spain, and, above all, Trotsky. I remember perfectly that when I was still a teenager, I dreamed of traveling to the Soviet Union. I longed to visit the country of the first victorious proletarian revolution and to see the Smolny, the Kremlin, and the Novo Dievichi Cemetery, where Trotsky, with snow beginning to fall in the dark, pronounced his last public speech on Soviet territory.

In 1974 it appeared that my dream might come true. I had been selected by a scientific committee and was ranked No. 1 on a list of candidates scheduled to spend some time in Moscow as an historian and researcher. But the Soviet authorities, without any explanation, invited Nos. 2, 3, 4—all the way up to No. 11—and kept silent about No. 1. Nonetheless, I had a chance to visit Czechoslovakia in 1967, Poland in 1981, and I consequently thought that a trip to Moscow, because of the present *glasnost* openings in the U.S.S.R., could become a possibility in 1989.

So I was not surprised when an old comrade of mine in the teachers' union, a socialist activist and great admirer of Mikhail Gorbachev, asked me on Oct. 4, 1988, if I would be willing to be part of a delegation to the Soviet Union—assuming the Soviet consulate granted me a visa. I said yes and alerted my Russian interpreter and translator for the Leon Trotsky Institute, Isabelle, who was enthusiastic about the prospects of

---

Professor Pierre Broué, noted historian and author, has just completed the most extensive biography to date of Leon Trotsky. He is the director of the Leon Trotsky Institute, which is based in Grenoble, France.

traveling to the Soviet Union.

I had to write my request for a visa and decided to openly tell the truth as a sort of test. I stated that I was a Trotskyist and a biographer of Trotsky. I added that I wanted to know if it would be possible to do some research on the Soviet Union and to talk to Soviet historians (I mentioned Yuri N. Afanasiev) about the recent changes and about ways of gaining access to the Soviet archives on Trotsky, his family, and his comrades of the Left Opposition. I specified that I wanted to meet witnesses of Trotsky's life and of the Trotskyists' persecution. Finally, I wrote that I wanted to find Trotsky's granddaughter, Aleksandra (Sasha) Sakhvalova, the half-sister of my good friend Esteban (Sieva) Volkov.

I was granted a visa. Nobody can say that it was by chance. I thought that I would be allowed to do whatever I intended to do.

I must state, however, that in the Soviet Union I had no access to the Soviet archives on Trotsky and the Left Opposition. I met Yuri Afanasiev, the director of the History and Archives Institute in Moscow, and tried to find out about new rules for consulting the archives. His answer was that there were no new rules: There had been no change of policy concerning the archives I was interested in; that is, the KGB Collection and the Stalin Collection.

It is interesting to note that no law, no rule, forbids consultation of these archives, yet only a privileged few are allowed to consult them. Two persons at least have been given access to the files: General Dimitri Volkogonov, Stalin's new official biographer, and leading playwright M. Shatrov, Gorbachev's friend and standard-bearer of *glasnost* in theater and historical plays.

Afanasiev was hopeful that these archives would be opened sometime in the near future—at least to people in charge of preparing new textbooks (after the old ones were so strongly condemned by the strike of the high-school students last year).

Meeting with Sasha

I was very fortunate to find Sasha, Trotsky's granddaughter. Sasha was the child of Trotsky's daughter Zinaida, known as Zina, and her first husband, Sakhar Moglin, who was a member of the Workers' Opposition and who was later shot in the 1930s. After a divorce, Zina married Platon I. Volkov, a communist teacher. Esteban Volkov was born from this marriage. Thus, Sasha is Sieva's half sister.

Isabelle and I spent several hours with Sasha. We found her very sick, sitting on her bed, with the breath of death already on her face. She was suffering from terminal cancer. (She died in her Moscow apartment on March 10, 1989, close to four months after my visit.) She grasped in her hand a photograph in which a baby boy is sitting on the knee of a little girl: She was with Sieva!

Sasha never saw Sieva again after his departure in 1931 from the Soviet Union with her mother, Zinaida, until his visit in 1988 just before she died. It was a very sad and very difficult visit with her. She has always known that she was Trotsky's granddaughter and that she had a brother somewhere "in America." She had also learned about her mother's death, but without any of the details.

It was difficult for me to describe under what conditions her mother had left the Soviet Union 58 years ago or how her mother had died 55 years ago.

I had to explain that her mother did not have to make a "Sophie's Choice," as Meryl Streep did in her famous film: Zinaida left with Sieva only because Stalin refused to let Sasha go with her and kept her in Soviet Russia somewhat like a hostage. [Zina contracted tuberculosis in 1931 and was allowed to travel to Berlin to seek a cure. But Stalin allowed her to take only one of her two children with her. She took Sieva, age 5, leaving Sasha, age 8, behind.—ed.]

I do hope that she was seriously relieved to learn that her mother had never decided to abandon her. Then I had to tell her how and why her mother, a young woman of 32 years, committed suicide in Berlin. This was a terrible moment for me because it involved telling her the whole story of Zina's nervous breakdown and then of her mental sickness. Telling this story I couldn't help but think that only animals are normally entitled to ignore the conditions, date, and reasons of their parents' death.

Sasha was not an animal, however, but a woman who lived under Stalinism. She had been exiled to Siberia, then sentenced to a labor camp. Following her release she married Anatoli Pakhvalov, a campmate. She became a chemist and raised her daughter, Olga, now 26. She decided only in September 1988 to declare to her friends that she was Trotsky's granddaughter, with the hope that it could allow her to find her brother—and it did. After visiting Sasha, profoundly moved, I called Sieva in Mexico. He came to Moscow in December. [See interview in this section with Sieva about his return to the Soviet Union.—ed.] Thus, before she died she was able to see her brother and clasp his hands in her own.

I saw Sasha smiling only once. I had asked about her cousins—Nina's and Serioja's children, raised along with her by the *babuchka* [grandmother], Aleksandra Sokolovskaya, until 1935. She answered that all of them were officially dead. But she always thought that Lev, Nina's son, may have been saved, given his intelligence and courage. She told me that in the children's gallows of the Stalinist camps there were two sorts of prisoners: the hooligans, protected by the guards but often killing one another; and the "Children of the Enemies of the People," who were beaten and oppressed by the guards and by the hooligans. The only chance for a boy to get out was to take the identity of a dead hooligan, and she thought that Lev had done that. She smiled—for the only time—and commented: "If so, he is now in some Siberian village not even knowing that there is a *perestroika*."

Frankly speaking, my encounter with Sasha was certainly one of the most painful but yet one of the most encouraging moments of my life.

The Memorial Meeting in Moscow

But perhaps the greatest moment of all for me was the Nov. 15, 1988, public rally of the group Memorial in Moscow. (That is where I met people who were later able to introduce me to Sasha.)

The day after our arrival, Isabelle and I were invited to have dinner with one of the most respected foreign correspondents of Moscow, a journalist with *Le Monde* whose father was a Trotskyist with me when we were young. The phone rang while we were eating. He answered and, smiling, told me, "It's for you." I couldn't believe I was receiving a phone call in Moscow.

I heard a female voice, speaking fluent French, who informed me that a meeting of Memorial was to be held the next day, that is, November 15, to demand Trotsky's rehabilitation, and that I was invited. The meeting was to be held in the Palace of Culture of the National Aeronautical Institute, familiarly called MAI by the Muscovites. The Memorial group is an independent nationwide organization that has spearheaded a campaign to erect a memorial monument with all the names of Stalin's victims engraved in stone. It has also organized to demand the creation of a library with the complete archives of Stalinist repression.

Four hundred tickets for the event had been sold 15 days in advance, even though no publicity had gone out, only word of mouth. The hall seated only 400 people. During the final week before the meeting, thousands of people had tried to get tickets—but in vain.

The night of the event, more than 1000 people were knocking at the doors of MAI, trying to get in. Five hundred people were finally allowed in. I didn't have a ticket, but holding up my book which had a picture of Trotsky on the cover page, I was ushered in and seated with Isabelle and my French friends in the front row.

At the entrance, there were large billboards with photos of Trotsky; his companion, Natalia Ivanovna Sedova; and Lev Sedov, his son and close collaborator. The billboards included information about Trotsky's role in Soviet history and his fight as the leader of the Left Opposition against Stalin and the party apparatus. People were literally jumping over each other to read the texts, those concerning Trotsky's Soviet period as well as his last exile from 1929 on.

The event was chaired by a young lecturer named V. Lyssenko. Speakers on the platform included S. Dzarasov, a philosopher; the historian Boulgakov; Yuri Heller, who is particularly well-informed about the civil war; as well as two children of renowned Bolshevik Party leaders.

One of them was Nadezhda A. Joffe, who is 82. She is the daughter of Adolf A. Joffe, Trotsky's personal friend and a leader of the Left Opposition who committed suicide as a political protest in 1927, when Stalin refused him permission to leave the country to get necessary medical care. Nadezhda, a childhood friend of Lev Sedov in Vienna, then Petrograd and Moscow, was a member of the Communist Youth. She was arrested and deported because of her militant opposition to the Stalinist bureaucracy. She was sentenced to hard labor in the infamous camps of Kolyma and Magadan.

The other child of a Bolshevik Party leader was Igor Ossipovitch Piatnitsky. Igor's father, a man of the underground, had been the treasurer of the Communist International. He was arrested in the 1930s and summarily shot. Igor had also been arrested. Along with Nadezhda and the others, he was one of the "Children of the Enemies of the People." Igor had become a human rights activist in the Memorial Group. He died from a heart attack several months after the Nov. 15 Memorial meeting.

The 500 people in the audience, except for us, were all Soviets. From their appearance and clothing it was obvious they were the average people one would encounter on the streets or in the metro—and not the privileged elite that drive around in their Volga limousines. There were a few old-timers and a few teenagers. (The security team was made up of high-school-age men and women, probably less than 18 years old.)

It soon became clear that there were also two very distinct groups in the room. The first group was comprised mainly of older white-haired women who sat in the first two rows of the hall. When they were introduced to the audience, we heard names that were the pride and glory of their parents' generation; names like Antonov-Ovseenko, Lomov, Lominadze, Smilga, Kretinsky, and many others. They, too, were "Children of the Enemies of the People." They came to give their own personal testimonies and to demand Trotsky's rehabilitation.

The other group, mostly men of about 30 to 40, were visibly angered, actually infuriated, by the call to rehabilitate Trotsky. These people were members of the right-wing Pamyat group, a group that ideologically is fascist but that is tolerated and even promoted by the KGB. At every possible opportunity, they got up to express their hatred for Trotsky, whom they described as "the Jew Trotsky," or "the murderer Trotsky," or "the executioner Trotsky." It was clear that for them Trotsky is the pseudonym of Lenin and generally speaking of the October Revolution—described by one of them as the "bloody utopia of socialism." Pamyat are Russian chauvinists who are violently hostile to the oppressed nationalities in the Soviet Union. They interrupted and tried openly to break up the meeting. They acted as direct agents of the KGB.

The main speakers of the event began their presentations by refuting the current attacks on Trotsky—and not just the old slanders of the Stalin era—according to which Trotsky was equivalent to Stalin and would have been at least as ruthless a dictator as Stalin had he won the "power struggle" against him.

They all responded to the countless lies published regularly even today in the Soviet press, basing themselves on their own experience and specialized knowledge. Boulgakov, the only historian on the platform, set the overall framework for the presentations and discussion. Yuri Heller refuted the old slander that depicts Trotsky massacring loyal Soviet Communist Party members while leading the Red Army during the Civil War. Piatnitsky said that the April Theses of Lenin were the admission that Trotsky was right about his theory of "Permanent Revolution." He, in fact, gave an excellent presentation on "permanent revolution"—even using a quote from Bukharin, who stated that the whole Bolshevik Party during the revolution and Civil War had adopted Trotsky's theory of the "permanent revolution."

Nadezhda Joffe, also on the speakers' platform, recounted childhood memories of going to school with Lev Sedov and sitting on Trotsky's lap. She remembered Trotsky as a kind and caring man. Was Stalin such a man? The audience laughed.

Then began questions and speeches at the open microphone that was placed in the auditorium. The Pamyat group tried to break up the meeting, but they were finally ejected, without the use of violence, for their disruptive activities.

Among others speaking from the floor were people of all ages and all walks of life. Somebody asked if it was true that Stalin allowed Trotsky to leave Russia with a train car full of gold when Stalin expelled him from the Soviet Union. But another was interested in such details as the different Spanish oppositionist groups in the 1930s.

One of the most powerful speakers was, without any doubt, Galina Antonov-Ovseenko, the daughter of the man who led the storming of the Winter Palace, was the political leader of the Red Army up until 1923, and was shot by Stalin in 1938. Galina spoke wih tremendous energy and passion. She said, "What is Trotskyism? It is my whole life, the October Revolution, my country itself." She continued, "Now it is time for us to demand our history. Give us back our history. We want truth, the whole truth."

Tatiana Smilga was another powerful speaker. She was moved when she evoked her youth, the ties between Trotsky and her parents, the admiration all of them had for Trotsky. Every word in her speech showed she was undaunted.

Other people asked questions relative to history. Why did Trotsky accuse Stalin of having poisoned Lenin when there is no evidence at all to back up this charge? Why did he refuse to defend the Georgian communists at the 11th Party Congress? Why was he not present at Lenin's funeral?

Boris Kagarlitsky, the well-known activist of the Moscow People's Front, while approving the rehabilitation of Nikolai Bukharin reminded the audience that Bukharin had helped Stalin to destroy the Left Opposition. He said that Trotsky's rehabilitation would mean much more than Bukharin's.

Many questions were asked of the speakers concerning their sources. "Where are the archives? Which documents exist? Who may read the archive documents? How can you prove what you say? How can you demonstrate that Stalinists are liars?"

Finally after more than four hours of meeting, Lyssenko, who was chairing the meeting, stood up and said they had done their best to answer the questions, but that the people on the platform, being Soviet citizens, could not answer questions relating to the archives. He added, "But today we are lucky. There is in the hall a man who is able to inform all of us about the Trotsky archives. The French historian Pierre Broué is here and I give him the floor."

"To My Great Surprise"

And so to my great surprise, here I was in Moscow, standing up before several hundred people, addressing a meeting on Trotsky. I was immediately helped in simultaneous translation by Nadezhda's daughter Larissa. I began by stating my name and saying I was a Trotskyist. I was immediately interrupted by thunderous applause. I added that I was a professor and an historian, and received an icy silence. It was not difficult for me to interpret this. Historians and professors in the Soviet Union have been associated with disseminating the Stalinist lies. They have a rotten reputation.

I explained that I had devoted over 30 years to researching the life and work of Trotsky. I told the true history of the archives from Moscow to Alma Ata, Alma Ata to Prinkipo, to France, to Norway, and finally to Mexico. I recounted how the bulk of Trotsky's archives had ended up in Harvard and how many original letters, including Sedov's archives, had ended up at the Hoover Institute at Stanford, with a part of these archives being deposited in Amsterdam. I explained what documents could be found in these archives: particularly the official documents, minutes, circulars, resolutions, and political correspondence between oppositionists. I mentioned the fascinating correspondence between deportees in the year 1928. I recalled Stalinist attempts to steal them, to destroy the archives, and how Trotsky decided to sell them for their own preservation.

I then showed a copy of my recently published biography of Trotsky, which is over 1100 pages in length and weighs close to three pounds, a comment that made everyone laugh. I said I had written this book not only for French readers but also for Soviet working people to help them in their struggle against what I called "the assassins of memory" who attempt to disfigure historical truth.

I added that I wanted to symbolically offer my book to the Soviet workers and youth, and that to do this I could do no better than to offer it to Nadezhda Joffe. And that's what I did.

Nadezhda grasped the book, waved it passionately over her head, and exclaimed loudly, "Never in my 82 years of life has a present meant so much to me and given me such great joy!" The audience responded with even louder applause.

The meeting then concluded with a vote of a resolution that called for Trotsky's rehabilitation, his reintegration into the Soviet Communist Party, the restitution of his Soviet citizenship, and the publication of all his works, Soviet as well as exile works.

After the meeting, I was immediately surrounded by dozens of people, old and young, who were exhilarated to meet a foreign Trotskyist and were thirsty to find out more about Trotsky. They gave me addresses, telephone numbers, words of friendship, and love. The daughter of an old Bolshevik murdered by Stalin gave me a kiss and said, "You are an old Bolshevik." I'm afraid I am not, but I will never forget her.

(Since that meeting, I received a very moving document from Vitali

Bronstein, Trotsky's grandnephew. This was a genealogy of the Bronstein family. Of 38 family members born before 1928, 36 were killed or died in prison.)

That Nov. 15, 1988, Memorial meeting was for me a day of joy and hope. I was lucky to be in Moscow in that room on that day. Returning to the Kosmos Hotel, I thought of the comrades from all countries who began the building of the Fourth International, following the International Left Opposition, and who all dreamed of living to see such a day. They would have relished seeing young Russian people with such passionate interest in Trotsky. They would have wept with joy seeing the courage and firmness of the Old Bolsheviks' children, who explained that for them the demand to rehabilitate Trotsky meant the defense of their parents and of the October Revolution.

During the following days, I tried to visit people who had invited me to their homes. I received in my hotel a group of high-school students who learned by word of mouth that I was Trotsky's historian and came to interview me. I met several people of the Moscow intelligentsia. I was impressed by the élan, the consciousness, and the enthusiasm of these people. When I asked questions about the Soviet workers, people generally answered that they were beginning to move forward and that the government was anxious not to antagonize them. It was reported that at the highest levels of the bureaucracy, they feared that a reform of retail prices could provoke social unrest, demonstrations, and strikes that would inevitably give birth to independent trade unions.

That fear was confirmed some weeks later by Shmeler, a top government official, in an interview with *Newsweek* magazine. (And as for the strikes and the calls to form independent unions, we had only to wait a few months.)

Before I left Moscow, I visited the Novo Dievichi Cemetery. Nadezhda Joffe had a new, beautiful, and simple gravestone done for her father. The snow began to fall in the dark. But the times have changed. We are now long after "midnight in the century."

Trotsky's Grandson Returns to the Soviet Union

Socialist Action: You just returned from a five-day trip to Moscow, your first trip back to the Soviet Union in 57 years. What was the purpose of your trip?

Esteban Volkov: In early December I got a phone call from Pierre Broué, who told me he had just returned from Moscow and that he had found my sister, Sasha [Aleksandra Sakhvalova, Volkov's half sister]. But he said that Sasha was deathly ill and would probably not live much longer. The next day, my wife Palmira and I went to the Soviet Embassy in Mexico City to request a visa to the Soviet Union. Three days later we got a call that our visa had been cleared in Moscow.

S.A.: What made you think that your sister was still alive after all these years?

Volkov: About 12 years ago, Lola Galin, who was a close collaborator of Leova [Leon Sedov, Trotsky's son] and who lived in New York at the time, sent me some review clips of a book by Olga Ivinskaya, who was Boris Pasternak's companion.

In her memoirs, Olga Ivinskaya mentions my sister. She said that when she was first sent to prison, she was placed in the same cell as a young woman who bore a striking resemblance to Lev Davidovich [Trotsky]. So she asked her if she was related to the "Old Man." The young woman said she was his granddaughter. The two women became good friends; it is a friendship that has remained to this day.

Over the past 10 years I repeatedly tried to find my sister, but to no avail. It was only about six weeks ago that Sasha decided to surface and declare publicly that she was Lev Davidovich's granddaughter.

S.A.: Tell us about your trip.

Volkov: When we arrived at the airport in Moscow, I was carrying some personal documents I had just picked up at a series of political events in Paris and Rome. When the customs authorities saw these materials, they took us aside, confiscated my documents, and summoned their

---

This interview with Esteban (Sieva) Volkov, grandson of Leon Trotsky, was conducted by Alan Benjamin, editor of **Socialist Action** *newspaper, on Dec. 23, 1988.*

superiors.

When the top authorities came over, they gave orders to return my confiscated belongings and they sent us on our way. Apparently *glasnost* has made some headway.

That same evening we went to my sister's place. You can imagine our joy to see each other. Even though her cancer is at an advanced stage, she was always smiling and full of optimism. [Sasha died on March 10, 1989, three months after Sieva's return to the Soviet Union.—ed.]

S.A.: According to Pierre Broué, she didn't know you were alive either.

Volkov: That's right. She said she had also tried to get information about me through the International Red Cross and other agencies. It seems hard to believe that she was never told about my whereabouts in Mexico. It is not as if I had been living anonymously.

S.A.: Tell us about your sister. According to Isaac Deutscher, she was imprisoned by Stalin in the mid-1930s with the other "Children of the Enemies of the People."

Volkov: Actually this is not what happened. Stalin decided to spare her life and to keep her as a sort of hostage. [When Zina, Trotsky's oldest daughter, contracted tuberculosis in 1931, she left for Berlin to seek a cure. But Stalin allowed her to take only one of her two children with her. She took Sieva, age 5, leaving Sasha, age 8, behind.—ed.]

Sasha was not detained until 1949. Prior to that she had lived with her paternal grandmother; that is, the mother of Sakhar Moglin, Zina's first husband. [Zina remarried a teacher named Platon I. Volkov two years after Sasha was born. With him she had one child, Sieva.—ed.]

After her detention, Sasha spent five months in jail. She was then sentenced to 10 years in exile in Khazakhstan Balchach. But with Stalin's death, that sentence was reduced to five years.

It is during her exile that she met her current husband, an engineer named Anatoli Pakhvalov, with whom she had a daughter, Olga, who is now 26. Olga has a boy who is 5 years old. Sasha herself is a chemical engineer.

S.A.: What is her view of her grandfather?

Volkov: I told her that one of my goals, one of my passions, is to see to it that the full truth about our grandfather be told, that his name be cleared, and that justice finally be done to the millions of innocent victims of this bloody Stalinist tyranny. She said she was fully in agreement with these views. She said she deeply admired Lev Davidovich.

S.A.: Did you meet any other people during your stay in Moscow?

Volkov: Yes. A film crew of the pro-Gorbachev monthly magazine

Ogonyok did a long interview with me about Lev Davidovich's last years in Mexico, and, for the first time, they interviewed my sister about her life's story.

We also met with the Memorial group. The organizers invited us to their office, the House of the People, where a large photo of Lev Davidovich was prominently displayed in the entrance. Under the photo was a big sign urging people to sign a letter that demanded Trotsky's rehabilitation.

Once there, I was asked to say a few words to a meeting of the group that happened to be taking place in an adjoining auditorium. I was told there were about 500 people present.

So I addressed the group and commended them for their magnificent work. Then, upon request, I gave a detailed account of my recollections of Lev Davidovich and answered many of their questions.

S.A.: How were your comments received?

Volkov: Very enthusiastically. I told them to continue their work and not to be sidetracked. They responded that ours was a common struggle.

Delegation from Trotsky's Family Visits the U.S.S.R.

By CARL FINAMORE

Pre-election campaign meetings, rallies, and demonstrations reached an unprecedented level on the eve of the March 26, 1989, national elections. A new election law passed last year made it possible, if still quite difficult, to nominate candidates who are not part of the government structures. Even the Communist Party (CPSU) daily newspaper, *Pravda,* reported that there would be complete freedom to campaign for these "unofficial" candidates.

This was the time chosen for a 10-day visit to Moscow by a delegation of U.S. Trotskyists—Susan Weissman, Paul Siegel, Ralph Schoenman, and myself. We were joined during the final days of our March 3-13, 1989, trip by Vlady Kibalchich, son of Victor Serge, a leader of the Left Opposition during the 1920s and '30s. [See highlights of the delegation's Moscow tour following this article.—**ed**.]

One of the main objectives of the trip was to deliver a letter to the Soviet authorities from the family of Leon Trotsky. The letter requested that Trotsky's name be cleared and that his works be published freely in the Soviet Union.

We quickly arranged a meeting with Otto Latsis, Deputy Editor of *Kommunist,* the theoretical journal of the Central Committee of the CPSU. Latsis agreed to give the letter to the CPSU Central Committee for discussion, but did not promise an official response from Soviet President Mikhail Gorbachev.

The delegation asked Latsis for his views on the prospects for Trotsky's rehabilitation. He said, "As far as Trotsky being a spy, a murderer of Kirov, etc.—in these cases his rehabilitation is inevitable. But as far as political rehabilitation—this is something else." Latsis did say, however, that Trotsky's works must begin to be published regardless of his rehabilitation.

We asked Latsis about recent Soviet articles that have been filled

---

Carl Finamore is a member of the National Committee of Socialist Action. He was the coordinator of the March 1989 trip to the Soviet Union by a delegation representing the families of Leon Trotsky and Victor Serge.

with slanders against Trotsky. In particular, we inquired about an article by General Dimitri Volkogonov, the official government biographer of Stalin. Latsis replied: "Even in Volkogonov's article there are some corrections from previous articles. Volkogonov reported facts on Trotsky's life which had been unpublished. This process will continue and we will get new information."

The "process" referred to by Latsis is tantamount to a second political assassination of Leon Trotsky. Volkogonov wrote that Trotsky was the "Demon of the Revolution" and would have been worse than Stalin. The Soviet bureaucracy wants to ensure that Trotsky is "politically" dead before they allow his "rehabilitation."

Every week, we were told, excerpts of Trotsky's writings or reports about Trotsky's views appear in *Pravda* and other major Soviet publications. These reports deal almost exclusively with the period of war communism during the civil war of 1918-21, when Trotsky called for the militarization of labor after his own proposals for an NEP-type program (limited concessions to the medium and large farmers) were rejected.

Certain problems were readily apparent. The presentation of Trotsky's views is being organized by his bitter political foes. The selection of excerpts, the failure to place them in the context of the party debates at the time, and the refusal to publish Trotsky's full views have greatly distorted Trotsky's role and ideas in the minds of many Soviet people today. We often encountered the view that Trotsky and even Lenin were the intellectual precursors of Stalinism. Of course, the bureaucracy still idealizes Lenin, but they continue to heap abuse, distortions, and attacks on Trotsky.

Meeting with Medvedev

One of our first meetings was with Roy Medvedev, the Marxist dissident who several weeks after our discussions was elected People's Deputy. Medvedev is a prominent historian who 20 years ago was expelled from the Communist Party for the publication in the West of his "Let History Judge," an analytical exposé of Stalinism. He is now an influential figure, and his book will soon be published in the Soviet Union. We were quite surprised to learn that he is writing an introduction to Isaac Deutscher's classic biography of Trotsky, which will also be published soon in the Soviet Union.

Medvedev told us he does not agree with Trotsky's ideas and that he supports *glasnost* and Gorbachev. But, as an historian, he said he completely opposes the current distortions of Trotsky's political views.

Medvedev, in fact, had already publicly attacked Volkogonov's false characterization of Trotsky.

Medvedev emphasized, however, that it remains very difficult for the Soviet leadership to clear Trotsky's name. He said that Trotsky's political positions were so antagonistic to the whole Stalinist machinery and the basic structure of the bureaucratized society that taking this step would be a major challenge for the regime. Nonetheless, he said, it was inevitable that some day Trotsky would be rehabilitated.

In an interview with our delegation, Medvedev said:

"In Stalin's time the god was Lenin. Stalin was his student, and the devil was Trotsky. . . . Trotsky and the Jews were blamed for the hardships of the revolution. People began to think that all the bad things from the revolution came because of Trotsky.

"Today, Trotsky has again been called the 'Demon of the Revolution.' But the real demon of the revolution is Stalin. The masses have heard nothing but lies about Trotsky for so long that the rehabilitation of Trotsky has many political problems.

"Today, with some of the articles on Trotsky, there's also an element of rehabilitation of Stalin: 'Stalin was a tyrant and repressed many people, but if Trotsky had come to power it would have been even worse.' This point of view is very widespread. I disagree with this view.

"The struggle around Trotsky is just beginning. In order to break free from these stereotypes we need time and preparation."

While most people we spoke to, like Medvedev, considered Trotsky's rehabilitation inevitable, it is my own view that it will be some time before this happens. It is not necessary for the bureaucracy to clear Trotsky's name now. It is only necessary to allow the mostly one-sided discussion about him to continue.

Whatever happens, it is obvious that the Left Opposition opponents of Stalin are not going to get a fair hearing if the presentation of their views remains in the hands of the ruling elite. Nonetheless, there are big openings for supporters of Trotsky to participate in the current discussions about the history of the anti-Stalinist opposition.

Meeting of Writers' Union

Almost immediately after our arrival, we identified ourselves not only as representatives of Trotsky's family but as political supporters of his views. We encountered absolutely no fear or apprehension on the part of people who talked to us. On the contrary, there was tremendous interest in what we had to say.

As a result of this approach we stumbled upon an important meeting we otherwise would have missed. People found out about us and said, "Oh you're Trotskyists, well you should go to the writers' meeting. It's going on right now!" They said this meeting was not all that unusual. They repeated what we had heard earlier from Medvedev, that there are regular seminars, panel discussions, and occasional articles in the press that raise the question of Trotsky's rehabilitation. The issue has even been debated on Soviet television.

A friend offered us his car, and we rushed to the Writers' Union meeting. There were 150 people present. The keynote speaker was Dr. Stuartsev, who gave a two-hour presentation on the need to clear Trotsky's name and the role Trotsky played in history. The talk was followed by lively discussion from the audience. At one point, a 106-year-old Red Army veteran got up to speak about his personal experiences with Trotsky.

We were greeted as representatives of the Trotsky and Serge families and were very warmly received. Vlady Kibalchich spoke in Russian from the podium in support of clearing his own name, the name of his father, Victor Serge, and Trotsky's name. Vlady was stripped of his Soviet citizenship when he and his father were expelled from the Soviet Union in 1936 after three years of internment.

The March 26 National Elections

Many aspects of the old Stalinist election law still exist. If you are a member of several official organizations you can vote many times. For example, if you're a member of the CPSU, the Academy of Science, the Writers' Union, and Komsomol (the CPSU youth organization)—you can vote four times for the "official" candidates of each organization. The average Soviet citizen gets to vote only once in the general election.

But there are two new democratic features to the election law which create big opportunities for dissident organizations to raise their own ideas independently of the bureaucracy.

First, the new election law permits electoral activity for candidates without the obligation of obtaining permits for activities. This is often violated by authorities, however. When we were in Moscow, five People's Front activists holding an election meeting were arrested for holding a street rally. They were charged with "interfering with a snow plow." The election law is by no means fairly enforced in practice.

We were asked by the five defendants to go to the trial. One of the activists was in the hospital because he had been beaten. Two of the people refused to recognize the trial and failed to appear. The two who showed up told us they were going to sue the city because they had been illegally prevented from having a meeting in support of a candidate. The proceedings were postponed until they could get an attorney.

These examples of resistance, and even open defiance, of arbitrary treatment reflected a level of rebelliousness that did not exist even two or three years ago.

The second democratic feature of the new election law is one that allows unofficial organizations to make nominations for candidates to the new supreme governing body: the Congress of U.S.S.R. People's Deputies. This means that in any one of the dozens of districts in Moscow a meeting of at least 500 people can make an unlimited number of nominations by majority vote.

The Moscow People's Front was able to get meetings of 500 people in most of that city's districts. This was a tremendous achievement. As a result, the People's Front grew considerably. In one district, activists told us how they rang doorbells and visited about 200 people a day to convince them to come to a meeting. This club soon grew from three people to 50 people.

Boris Kagarlitsky, a leader of the 40-member Socialist Initiative Club, estimates that the People's Front has 2000 to 3000 people in Moscow. It is the most advanced and largest unofficial political organization in the city.

The People's Front nominated four of its own candidates in these district meetings and supported other candidates as well. It supported former Moscow regional CPSU chief Boris Yeltsin, for example.

The second stage of the elections, however, is where the CPSU begins to assert its bureaucratic control by screening out the candidates. Electoral commissions exist in each district to screen all the candidates to determine which ones will be on the final ballot. The electoral commissions are dominated by CPSU representatives.

As a result, of the four People's Front candidates, only Sergei Stankevich, a leader of the Moscow People's Front and a CPSU member, made it through this second stage. He was subsequently elected as a People's Deputy. It is testimony to the growing strength of opposition forces that they were able to make substantial gains despite the many obstacles.

People's Front Conference

We were present at the pre-founding conference of the Moscow People's Front on March 11-12, 1989. There were 55 delegates present from the 34 constituent clubs and about 100 guests.

The conference began with a discussion over the composition of the presiding committee. At the very beginning something occurred which showed the wide appeal of the People's Front. A lieutenant colonel in the army took the floor and stated why he should be elected to the presiding committee.

The officer joined the People's Front three days before the conference and said, "I am being repressed in the military because I am taking it upon myself to defend the families and the soldiers who are being demobilized from Eastern Europe and Afghanistan and are entering civilian life without any protection." He was elected overwhelmingly to the presiding committee.

There was also a debate on whether to have someone from the Russian Federation Club be part of the presiding committee. The nominee was a Russian nationalist who came under strong criticism because of his views, which many people considered anti-Semitic. He had previously condemned all the Jewish leaders of the People's Front by name.

The Russian Federation Club, according to Boris Kagarlitsky, is not as extremist in its views as Pamyat, the openly reactionary, anti-Semitic, Russian chauvinist organization. However, the club did publish a Pamyat statement without comment, which led to a big uproar at the conference.

But even those who condemned this person for his views, with the exception of Kagarlitsky, did not want the person expelled. It appeared to me that, at least in this instance, the extreme tolerance of different opinions that exists among the intellectuals in the People's Front is an exaggerated reflection of their complete rejection of Stalinist repression. The Russian Federation leader was not only elected to the presiding committee, but to the Coordinating Council, the seven-person leadership body.

One of the main controversial debates at the conference was whether to adopt resolutions that were either hostile or conciliatory to the CPSU. Whereas Kagarlitsky was for expelling the member from the Russian Federation Club, he was unwilling, when it came to a major programmatic question, to take a clear position. He considered the two motions—to be hostile or conciliatory to the CPSU—to be a provocation, because the adoption of either motion would have split the People's Front membership. We were told that approximately 20 percent of the People's Front members are also CPSU members.

The People's Front program calls for socialist democracy, ecology, human rights, democratic reforms, self-management, and an end to price increases—but there is no fundamental political challenge to *perestroika*.

The front's full name, the People's Front in Support of Perestroika, reflects its orientation. The intellectuals and professional workers in the People's Front favor *perestroika* market reforms because they confuse these reforms with democracy and participation in economic decision-making. Their goal is limited to lessening the damaging effects that *perestroika* austerity reforms will have on the population.

The People's Front pre-founding conference did not, therefore, offer alternative proposals of democratic planning, free trade unions, or the unrestricted right to strike. These urgent and necessary political planks are absent in both the statement of intentions of the Socialist Initiative Club, which is a more advanced Marxist club, and in the program of the People's Front as a whole.

Perhaps the central debate at the conference was whether to have the 34 clubs remain relatively autonomous or whether to adopt a more centralized coordinating committee. Those clubs that wanted to carry out their own political projects wanted to retain the decentralized character of the front. The so-called Kagarlitsky program calling for the election of a central leadership body won overwhelmingly by 44 to 10.

Discussion with Kagarlitsky

But a question arises. With the broadly formulated program of the People's Front and the widely divergent views of its component parts, is it in a position to act effectively and will it be able to maintain its political independence from the reform wing of the bureaucracy?

We discussed this question with Kagarlitsky and asked about the alternative of organizing united-front coalitions on broad issues such as democratic election reform, strike solidarity, and the defense of political prisoners while building a political organization on a more defined program than that of the People's Front. Kagarlitsky didn't think this approach was correct. He defended the all-inclusive membership and general program of the Moscow People's Front, believing that this would give the group greater tactical flexibility.

Boris Kagarlitsky's Socialist Initiative Club is a Marxist group within the People's Front, though you do not have to be a Marxist to be a member. It does not really have a program itself; it has a statement of intention. Thus, even though it has more political definition, it closely follows the vague and broad political approach of the People's Front as a whole.

Despite the questions we were left with, the contributions of the Socialist Initiative Club must be recognized as very important. It was Kagarlitsky, for example, who got the People's Front to adopt a position on socialist democracy, whereas many people did not even want the word socialist in the program. Some also just wanted economic—and not political reform mentioned in the program.

But without an approach toward the Soviet working class around clear demands for workers' control of production, mass democratic control of distribution, the right to strike, the right to form independent unions, and the freedom to form political parties, both the People's Front and the Socialist Initiative Club run the risk of being isolated from the only powerful section of society that has the power to defeat the bureaucracy and fulfill the original goals of the Russian Revolution.

HIGHLIGHTS OF THE TOUR

• Presented letter from the family of Leon Trotsky to Otto Latsis, Deputy Editor of *Kommunist*, the theoretical journal of the Communist Party of the Soviet Union (CPSU). Latsis promised to present the letter to the Central Committee of the CPSU. Also did extensive interview with Latsis.

• Susan Weissman and Vlady Kibalchich obtained agreement of the Soviet Foundation of Culture to aid in the search for the lost manuscripts of Victor Serge. These manuscripts were stolen from Serge as he was expelled from the Soviet Union in 1936.

• Attended a meeting of the Moscow Writers' Union on the subject of clearing Leon Trotsky's name. The delegation was warmly greeted by the audience of 150. Vlady Kibalchich, son of Left Oppositionist Victor Serge, addressed the meeting.

• Attended a meeting of 2500 to support the candidacy of Boris Yeltsin, a veteran member of the ruling bureaucracy who has cultivated a populist image in recent years.

• Attended a mass outdoor meeting of Memorial of several thousand people held on the March 5 anniversary of Stalin's death. Memorial was formed to expose the crimes of Stalin and to seek compensation for the survivors of the repression.

• Attended the pre-founding conference of the Moscow People's Front, the largest unofficial political group in that city.

• Extensive interview and discussions with Boris Kagarlitsky, leader of the Socialist Initiative Club and of the Moscow People's Front.

• Extensive interview with 106-year-old Alexander Davidovich Brianski, a veteran of the 1905 and 1917 revolutions, who spoke in defense of Trotsky at the Writers' Union meeting.

- Meeting with Nadezhda Joffe and family.
- Extensive interview and discussion with Marxist historian and dissident Roy Medvedev.
- Distributed many classic works of Trotsky in Russian and presented a copy of the *Bulletin of the Left Opposition* to the historian of the group Memorial.
- Attended the trial of five arrested People's Front activists. They were tried for "unauthorized election activity."
- Extensive interviews of the Trotskyist delegation by several newspapers, including the *Moscow News*, the Moscow University newspaper, the Moscow CPSU youth newspaper, a Moscow regional district paper called *Avantgard*, and a Baltic region newspaper. *Komsomolskya Pravda*, the CPSU national youth paper, also interviewed Susan Weissman and Vlady Kibalchich on the life and works of Victor Serge. Moscow TV requested an interview but was unable to arrange it before our departure. Arrangements were made to interview Vlady Kibalchich, who remained in Moscow for 10 more days.

March 5, 1989, Memorial rally of several thousand in Moscow's Gorky Park calling for expansion of democratic rights. Sign reads: "The crimes of Stalin are crimes against humanity."

Moscow citizens rally to condemn Stalin's crimes on March 5—the anniversary of Stalin's death in 1953.

Pierre Broué addresses Nov. 15, 1988, meeting of the Memorial Group in Moscow. Behind him other speakers look through Broué's biography of Trotsky.

Isabelle Broué

Moscow audience listens to candidates at election meeting in March 1989. Meeting halls were filled to capacity during election campaign.

Ralph Schoenman/Socialist Action

Sergei Stankevich speaks at a spontaneous soap-box rally outside a Boris Yeltsin election meeting. (Far right) Ralph Schoenman tried to tape everything. Carl Finamore/Socialist Action

Carl Finamore/Socialist Action

One of three rows of bureaucrats (apparatchiks) who walked out of the March 4, 1989, Boris Yeltsin election rally in a huff

(Left to right) Suzi Weissman, Boris Kagarlitsky, Carl Finamore, and Ralph Schoenman discuss results of People's Front Conference.

Paul Siegel (left) and an interpreter (right) speak with a woman, a Bukharin supporter, who survived imprisonment under Stalin. Her husband was shot and her child died in a labor camp orphanage.

February 14, 1989
Mexico, D.F., Mexico

To whom it may concern:
To the Government of the Soviet Union,

The participants in this study group—Carl Finamore, Vlady Kibalchich, Ralph Schoenman, Paul Siegel, and Susan Weissman—will be traveling shortly to the Soviet Union, where they hope to observe and learn more about the changes under way in that country.

The aforementioned all have close ties of friendship with the signer of this letter, Esteban Volkov, and with his daughters (grandson and great-granddaughters respectively of the Russian revolutionary Lev Davidovich Bronstein, better known as Leon Trotsky), which is why they have been entrusted to take our petition, addressed to His Excellency President Mikhail Gorbachev, to the highest Soviet authorities.

In this petition we ask that my grandfather, Leon Trotsky, be officially cleared of the calumnies and false accusations leveled against him under orders of Joseph Stalin, and that the prohibition on the publication of his writings be lifted so that they may be freely published in the Soviet Union.

With our most profound respect, we ask the Soviet authorities to please extend to the participants of this study group all the help and support they will require to fulfill the mission that has been entrusted to them by the descendants of Leon Trotsky, given the unquestionably extraordinary and historic character of their task.

Very sincerely,

Esteban (Vsievolod) Volkov

Esteban Volkov
Apdo. 21945
Mexico, 21, D.F..

Next two pages: copies of letters presented by the delegation on behalf of the families of Leon Trotsky and Victor Serge to Otto Latsis, Central Committee member of the Communist Party (CPSU).

To His Excellency Mr. Mikhail Sergeyevich Gorbachev
President of the Presidium of the Supreme Soviet
of the Union of Soviet Socialist Republics
Kremlin
Moscow, U.S.S.R.

We the undersigned—Vsievolod Volkov Bronstein, Veronica Volkow Fernandez, Nora Dolores Volkow Fernandez, Patricia Volkow Fernandez and Natalia Volkow Fernandez—grandson and great granddaughters respectively of the Russian Revolutionary Marxist Lev Davidovich Bronstein, better known as Leon Trotsky, write you, with all due respect, to ask that our grandfather and great-grandfather, his family, and his comrades in struggle be officially cleared of all the slanders and false criminal charges that were leveled against them under direct orders from Joseph Stalin.

We ask that the historical truth be fully brought to light concerning both the fundamental role played by Leon Trotsky, alongside Vladimir Lenin, in the development and triumph of the October Revolution, and the unequal and heroic struggle he waged against the Stalinist dictatorship—to the point of losing his life—in order to preserve the essential Marxist-Leninist postulates of the October Revolution.

We also request that the writings of Leon Trotsky, which constitute a valuable compilation of historical and contemporary Marxist teachings, be freely published in the Soviet Union.

You have written that the Soviet Union must find its way back to the ideals and foundations of Leninism. This is very necessary.

But for this to be accomplished, it is vital to uproot and discard forever the criminal methods of Stalinism so that the word socialism can never again be associated with totalitarianism, but rather with the fullest freedoms and authentic democracy. Only then will the Soviet Union once again stand as an example and beacon for humankind.

Sincerely,
Mexico City, December 30, 1988

Vsievolod Volkov Bronstein

Verónica Volkow Fernández

Nora Dolores Volkow Fernández

Patricia Volkow Fernández

Natalia Volkow Fernández

Muscovites at the March 5 anti-Stalin rally — Carl Finamore/Socialist Action

Paul Siegel/Socialist Action

Nadezhda Joffe (second from left) and her son-in-law (right) receive a photo book about Trotsky from delegation members Suzi Weissman (left) and Carl Finamore (second from right).

Rod Holt

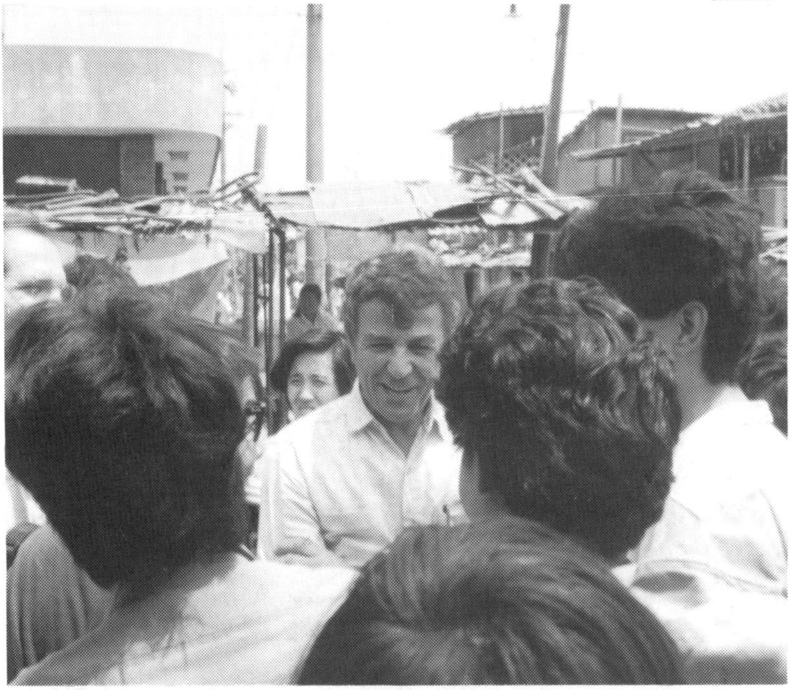

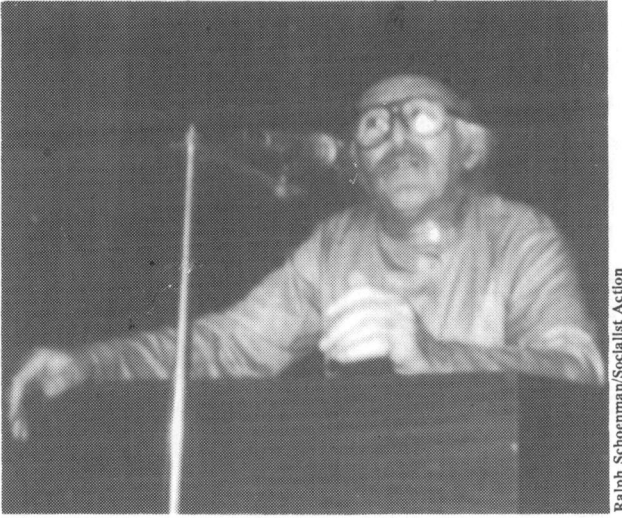

Nat Weinstein talks with Chinese workers and students in Shanghai during a 10-day visit in June 1989. Weinstein and other American socialists arrived shortly after the June 4 masssacre in Beijing.

Ralph Schoenman/Socialist Action

Vlady Kibalchich speaks at Writers Union meeting during socialist delegation trip to Soviet Union.

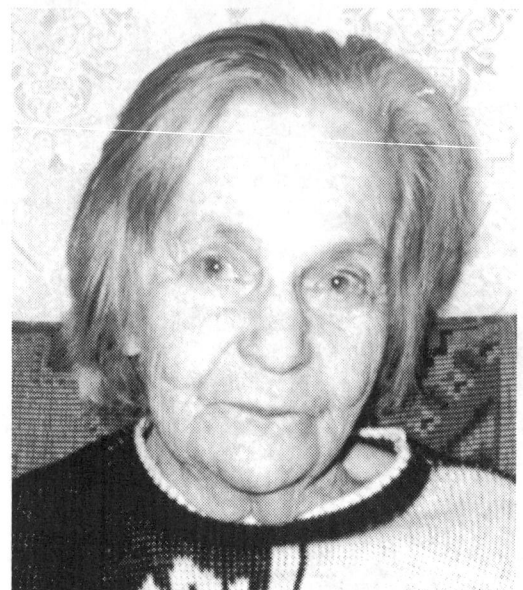

Nadezhda Joffe — Carl Finamore/Socialist Action

Roy Medvedev — Carl Finamore/Socialist Action

Leon Trotsky in 1939

Esteban Volkov

Joe Ryan/Socialist Action

Young Sieva (Esteban Volkov) with Trotsky and Natalia Sedova in Mexico in 1939.

Esteban Volkov, Trotsky's grandson, speaking at Aug. 6, 1988, rally celebrating the 50th anniversary of the Fourth International.

Greetings to Moscow People's Front Conference

On March 11-12, 1989, the delegation of U.S. Trotskyists who traveled to Moscow on behalf of the family of Leon Trotsky attended the pre-founding conference of the Moscow People's Front, the largest unofficial political group in that city. Greetings to this conference were presented on behalf of Socialist Action and the delegation itself. The following are excerpts from these greetings.

Greetings from Socialist Action

We come here today to present congratulations and warmest fraternal greetings from Socialist Action in North America to you, our comrades of the People's Front of the Soviet Union on the occasion of your pre-founding Congress.

Socialism, as a vision of justice and the most complete workers' democracy, has suffered incalculable harm at the hands of Stalin and the bureaucratic dictatorship he imposed on the peoples of the Soviet Union.

It is not just the blood of countless millions of people and the physical liquidation of the Bolshevik leaders which has stained the revolution. It is the false association of socialism with autocracy, privilege, corruption, crude chauvinism, and open sabotage of self-determination for oppressed nations within the Soviet Union.

There is an awesome responsibility to restore socialist democracy, workers' control of production, freedom for ideas, and democratic control of planning by working people in their factories, farms, and social institutions and in all elected bodies.

Now as in the past this is an international task. We in North America salute you and offer full participation and solidarity in our common struggle.

Moscow,
March 12, 1989

Greetings from the Delegation

We come to Moscow on behalf of the families of Leon Trotsky and Victor Serge, two of the seminal figures of the 20th century. They have been honored throughout the world as men who have shaped the moral, intellectual, cultural, and political life of our era. . . .

It was, however, the people of your country who produced them. The working people of Russia gave rise to these great men. Who then can deny that it is long overdue for Leon Trotsky and Victor Serge to be restored to the peoples of the Soviet Union to whom they belong?

We come here in the conviction that the day has arrived when working people in the Soviet Union will once again read, discuss, organize and, yes, fight openly for the ideas of these men, ideas forged in the furnace of revolutionary conviction. Leon Trotsky and Victor Serge embody the never-ending battle against exploitation, oppression, political enslavement, and, under its infinite disguises, the rule of the lie.

Thus, comrades, we come to you on behalf of the families of two of your own great leaders whose ideas must be heard here, no matter the consequences for those who have usurped power. We call out for the restoration of their good name, for the recovery of their rightful role in your history. . . .

Thank you comrades for the warmth of your reception. We salute you on behalf of Leon Trotsky and Victor Serge, who embody the best of your past and who remain, we feel certain, not only an integral part of your present valiant struggle, but beacons of a glorious future.

Moscow,
March 12, 1989

Boris Yeltsin Rally Reveals Deep Ferment

By RALPH SCHOENMAN

When our delegation arrived in Moscow carrying a letter to the Soviet leadership from the family of Leon Trotsky, we were unprepared for the intensity of oppositional ferment and the readiness with which people spoke of the need to transform and even replace the regime.

No one was under any illusion that the limited elections on March 26 were intended by those in power to permit effective challenge to the Communist Party of the Soviet Union (CPSU) and state machine. But all were prepared to seize the moment. The fervor with which people spoke of repression, endemic corruption, chronic shortages of the most basic necessities, endless lines, and the scale of privilege for party and state functionaries was matched by a sense of determination that this time there would be no turning back.

"Anything is possible in this dangerous country," said our 17-year-old interpreter, Artyom Artyomovich, "but if they try to shut down the opposition now, there will be civil war."

The elections added urgency to the prevailing mood. Artyom was a member of the newly formed Moscow People's Front with whose leaders, notably Boris Kagarlitsky, we were in daily contact. The People's Front was preparing its pre-founding conference and we were to attend. But for now, the nightly election meetings were an adventure.

Much interest centered on the fate of Boris Yeltsin, the former head of the Moscow CPSU and member of the Political Bureau who had been removed in November 1987. Nominated in over a dozen districts by supporters who saw Yeltsin's fight within the bureaucracy as an opening for broader and deeper protest, Yeltsin was astonished by the support he found in a public hungry for an avenue of challenge to the regime. He decided to run in the most prestigious arena, the at-large territorial district representing Moscow as a whole.

His opponent, Yevgeny Brakov, personified the Stalinist insider as a

---

Ralph Schoenman is the past Executive Director of the Bertrand Russell Peace Foundation. In 1982 he organized "American Workers and Artists for Polish Solidarnosc" to protest martial-law rule.

director of the factory making Zil limousines, the black chariots of the party elite. Yeltsin's successor as Moscow party chief, Lev N. Zaikov, regularly attacked Yeltsin as did party publications and functionaries. Each attack brought Yeltsin new support.

The regime sought to withhold permits for meetings, to cancel meeting halls previously booked for Yeltsin rallies, and to control the audience attending these events by issuing tickets to Yeltsin organizers at the last minute.

One consequence of this tactic was to prevent the general public from attending the meetings, as Yeltsin organizers made tickets available to those already known to them. But the people would learn of the meetings and show up in numbers larger than the seats available inside the meeting halls.

Soap-Box Rally

We drove to a Yeltsin meeting on a cold March night and found a crowd of several thousand milling around outside the hall. Spontaneous soap-box rallies were erupting everywhere. The People's Front candidates were addressing the crowd, who shouted questions and interrupted with lists of grievances and denunciations of the regime.

Sergei Stankevich, a member of the CPSU and a candidate for the People's Front, spoke spontaneously and engaged in heated debate with an enthusiastic crowd. "How can you fight this party Mafia, Sergei, if you are a member of it," shouted a middle-aged woman.

"The press has awakened the people," he tells the crowd, "and the People's Front opposes bureaucratic privilege, arbitrary rule, and the old ways." Stankevich tells us it is necessary to work inside the party to win over sections of its youth and to give critical support to Yeltsin. He says that the attacks must be concentrated on the "conservatives" in the party who "oppose *glasnost* and the press." The crowd is sympathetic to Stankevich but quick to challenge his assumption that the party can be an instrument of change.

Using press cards, we are able to get into the Yeltsin meeting, running a gauntlet of guards checking for tickets. We manage to get into the main hall, an enormous auditorium with a balcony, which alone holds some 2500 people. In the middle of the stage is a table where the meeting's organizers are seated together with the chairperson.

Yeltsin Feels His Way

Yeltsin is attacking Ligachev, the Stalinist member of the Political Bureau who opposes Gorbachev. Ligachev, Yeltsin tells the audience, is an unreconstructed opponent of *glasnost*, of popular participation in the political process, of the awakening sweeping the Soviet Union.

Yeltsin is surprisingly pedestrian as a speaker. Slow, methodical, unemotional, and rather monotone, he seems to be feeling his way. The atmosphere in the audience is dramatically different. People are leaning forward in their seats, reacting with asides and shouting out comments to Yeltsin: "What newspapers are you reading, which ones do you favor?"

Yeltsin interrupts his prepared remarks to respond, citing *Novy Mir*, *Yunost*, *Ogonyok*, and *Znamiya*, but not *Nash Sovremennik*. He has mentioned publications that support *glasnost* and pointedly omitted a conventional party organ. Now a member of the audience shouts out "*Ogonyok* may be liberal but they won't publish you!"

Yeltsin finds himself in a give-and-take with his audience, and his set speech has instead become an attempt to respond to the aggressive but critical and irreverent support from the hall. He is becoming more personal, human, and relaxed—and he proceeds:

"Korotich [the editor of *Ogonyok*] promised me he would publish their interview with me but later informed me there were 'personal problems.' When I asked what they were, I couldn't get an answer but I found out that it's because my wife uses the normal shops."

This gets a roar of approval from an audience familiar with the special shops for the party elite. The chairperson is getting restless and confers with Yeltsin. Yeltsin decides to walk from the podium to the table with his organizers and sit facing the audience to field their questions. This in itself is unusual as questions are normally required to be in writing, allowing the chair to pick and choose among them.

Microphone in the Aisle

A microphone is set up in the aisle. People crowd around it to fire questions. "You were Minister of Housing, comrade Yeltsin. How come the Ministry didn't carry out your orders?"

Yeltsin becomes animated: "Because my enemies are strong, because they pervade every ministry and drag their feet over every change for the better. If you knew how violent are my fights with Ligachev and the apparatus which supports him, you would be frightened. You can't imagine the mentality of these people."

"Yes, we can!" a voice booms out from the balcony. Yeltsin now speaks of the necessity for a five-year plan of reform that must be carried out if the system is to be workable. But before he can finish the thought a member of the audience takes the aisle microphone. "How do you expect to do that with one party? What about a multi-party system, comrade Yeltsin?"

"Society," says Yeltsin, "is not ready for the creation of a new party. This process is only now unfolding in our society. We must open the bureaucratic filter for this to happen."

There is silence in the hall. Yeltsin hesitates and then continues, "The possibility of many parties should be discussed in all the media and before the entire population. Society must be prepared to solve this problem." There is shouting and applause in the hall. Yeltsin adds, "I am not *against* a multi-party system." People now shout encouragement from all parts of the audience.

The flow between Yeltsin and the audience is clear. He improvises in response to them and is being pushed along by the intensity of feeling and a radical impulse he seeks both to contain and to represent.

People now speak about the national demands for self-rule, and Yeltsin is asked his opinion. He replies that he believes in working with the Republics. He states that he supports the People's Fronts in Latvia, Lithuania, and Estonia and sees no contradiction between national expression and the democratic demands of the People's Fronts. He says that supporting this will prevent people from turning to nationalism per se.

Yeltsin now declares that there are two wings to the state machinery—"the bureaucrats and progressive thinking people"—and he urges the audience to support him and oppose the others. There is mild applause.

"Let Us Decide"

At this point the chairperson proposes that questions should be sent up in writing. The audience erupts, "Let us decide!" "We should speak directly, not through you."

Yeltsin intervenes to support people coming to the microphone. "The people should decide things," he says. He is asked about the prosecutor, Gdlyan, who has indicted corrupt officials. "What about the Mafia which runs our economy?" someone asks. Yeltsin speaks in general terms about the need to overcome corruption while people are yelling out that speculators run the real economy.

The meeting is rapidly becoming a public forum. Speaker after speaker takes the microphone, but now from the stage itself. One speaker attacks Yeltsin from the right. "Why do you attack our state and party?"

The audience begins a rhythmic applause, drowning out the speaker. Yeltsin holds up his hand, silencing the audience, and comments: "Because the highest machinery of control, the state bureaucracy sits on top of our people like a dead weight." Thunderous applause echoes through the hall.

Yeltsin now warns, "There are many Komsomol [CPSU youth organization] and party apparatchiks sent into our meetings. Expect provocations from them such as questions about my contradictions with Mikhail Gorbachev, my tactical differences. I am against such methods. Only our enemies avoid stating our views accurately."

Yeltsin tries to align himself with Gorbachev and to attribute presumptive differences to their mutual opponents. A speaker from the aisle asks Yeltsin about his attitude toward private property. He states, "Our attitude is wrong. We must discuss private property. If a farmer buys a tractor and uses it for public purposes, that does not make it private. Don't call it private property. I'm against exploitation by owners."

Asked about his differences with Brakov, his opponent in the elections, he calls Brakov his enemy and describes how when he gave a speech on division within the party, Brakov managed to cut his remarks from a Canadian broadcast. "We must have more democratic discussion in this society."

"We Should Meet in Red Square"

There is a line forming now to use the microphones, and the chairperson proposes that there should be no more comments from the floor. There is an outcry from the audience and someone yells out, "We should be having meetings like this in the Palace of Congresses and in Red Square."

People start to approach the stage. Yeltsin stands up now and seizes the microphone, intoning in a loud voice, "You are right to speak from this platform. Stand up. People stand up. Don't be afraid of the bureaucrats. Speak openly. We must learn the culture of discussion!" The audience cheers him. His face is flushed.

One person yells out to Yeltsin, "Comrade Yeltsin, could Ligachev answer such questions?" "I hope so," Yeltsin answers. Now a person comes up to the stage and faces Yeltsin, asking, "Fifteen thousand people get 10 tickets. Who is isolating you from the people?" Yeltsin turns to the chairperson and says, "You must answer to them. You explain it."

A questioner now asks Yeltsin to tell the audience what the party budget is and Yeltsin replies that the party budget should be open to every member. "The CPSU must not be a collection of people paying dues but a group of individuals who have ideas and whose ideas are openly debated."

Another speaker asks Yeltsin sarcastically if it is ethical for the highest echelons of power to be "living under conditions of communism while speaking of 'reforming socialism?'"

Yeltsin answers:

"The first action I took upon assuming the position of first secretary of the party in Moscow was to remove every placard proclaiming Moscow to be a communist city. Then I took away all chauffeured cars from the bureaucrats and closed the special shops. It lasted one week! Our first problem is to democratize the CPSU. The number of candidates alone shows there is no democracy in the CPSU. In many cities and districts there are 100 people nominated for 100 seats. The local party cells provided 3100 candidates. The Komsomols picked 102 candidates for 75 seats."

Yeltsin's entire demeanor and manner of speech have changed. There is a current flowing back and forth now between him and the audience, and one can feel that something is taking place that is surprising Yelstin himself. The audience feels it too, and the questions take on an almost intimate tone.

"Why did you leave the Political Bureau. Why didn't you fight to stay?" Yeltsin replies, "Things were so hard it was impossible for me to continue. I *had* to leave. I could not change my principles as Ligachev and others demanded of me. My name became taboo in the mass media for one year."

Many people now come to the microphone to express support for Yeltsin. "Bring more Yeltsins. Organize support for him. Let's control the counting of votes so they don't steal the election. The mere fact of a Yeltsin victory will mean the bureaucracy is losing control over our people." It is a theme repeated for the next half-hour. Yeltsin has broken through to people.

"Bring Them All to Justice!"

Now a speaker stands up and criticizes anarchy and chaos. There is anger in the hall. People try to drown out the speaker. But many others shout that they must answer the apologists, not silence them. The next speaker calls for putting party and state leaders on trial for their criminal repression of the people. "Bring them all to justice." There is thunderous applause.

The next speaker declares that he represents the city of Dnepropetrovsk where, he states, the Mafia is stronger than it is even in Moscow. The chairperson nervously states that only Muscovites should speak in the meeting. There is an explosion of anger from the audience.

The speaker continues, "Ours remains the party of Brezhnev, Sholokov and Tcherbitsky [the latter is a Brezhnev holdover and party boss in the Ukraine; Sholokov was the corrupt Minister of the Militia who killed himself.] Comrades, we must create another party in order to control the CPSU." There is vast applause.

Now a worker takes the microphone and states, "Three years ago we Muscovites associated our hopes for change, for *perestroika*, with Yeltsin. Do not make idols of our leaders," he shouts while facing Yeltsin. "If we do, we shall wind up with 1937, not 1991. We support you, Yeltsin, but critically and with our eyes open." There is prolonged applause, and Yeltsin nods his approval to the speaker.

An older man stands up and says, "The new Congress of Deputies should make regular evaluations of every minister. They should be graded. Any who don't work in the interest of the working people should be kicked out."

An elderly woman follows him to the microphone and states, "I am a common person. I want to tell you that *Pravda* equals prostitution. When people from this so-called government say 'We are giving you democracy, why don't you act,' it is like saying to people without legs, 'We have an orchestra, why don't you march?'" Laughter and cheers fill the hall.

"We Have Built a Terror State"

The next speaker tells the audience, "The central issue is this. When someone earlier spoke about the Mafia running Moscow, the apparatchiks in the audience jumped. We know who you are and why you are in this hall. But you can't intimidate us anymore!"

"Ordinary communists," says the next speaker, "will not support the handpicked deputies of the party apparatus. The people decided on the political rehabilitation of Boris Yeltsin by nominating him."

"Our society," states the following speaker, "must be a constitutional society. We must remove from the constitution the words that in the Soviet Union we have developed socialism. We all know this isn't true. And remove the words of Article 6, which state that the CPSU plays the leading role in society. We have no Communist Party. We have 20 million people who pay dues and have no control."

The next speaker turns to Yeltsin and says, "Let's tell the plain truth. We haven't built a socialist society. We have built a terror state. If you speak out, Yeltsin, you will fulfill our hopes."

Now a young apparatchik takes the microphone and begins to attack Yeltsin for opening up the mass media. "The means of communication," he states, "must remain under the party's control. This should not be given to just anybody. That is dangerous for both the party and society."

The audience begins a rhythmic applause to drown him out. People yell out "provocateur!" Others protest the audience response, declaring, "Don't fall into their trap. Let them speak. We must know the views of the enemies of *perestroika*." Others try to drown out those criticizing the attempts to silence the former speaker.

One speaker now says, "When you act like this, you undermine the democratic views of Yeltsin." Another speaker, a member of the party, shouts into the microphone, "Silencing others is the provocation."

Now the chairperson appeals to the audience, "Allow people to speak in the spirit of *glasnost* and democracy." Yeltsin takes the microphone, "Let's listen to everyone—and answer them when necessary."

The next speaker says, "If there is any attempt to halt our campaign for democracy, we must organize a general strike. If Gorbachev is removed, we must act. We must make laws to prevent Gorbachev from being removed."

Artyom, our interpreter, yells from the audience, "What about when Gorbachev changes his mind and begins repression as he already did with the Karabakh Committee?" [The Karabakh Committee is the leadership body of the Armenian nationalist movement that is currently detained in a Moscow jail.] Many now support Artyom's remarks. A pensioner asks people who intend to vote for Yeltsin to raise their hands. Another speaker states, "If Yeltsin doesn't win, the People's Front is waiting for him to join."

"We Shall Expose You All"

The next speaker urges people to write in Yeltsin's name wherever there is only one candidate. Now a man in his thirties takes the microphone and informs the audience, "I am a former worker in the regional party committees. I was critical. I am now unemployed. Let's cut out the bullshit. I see the very KGB and apparatchik controllers of the regional party committees. I will name them for you."

He proceeds to reel off their names while pointing to rows 8, 9, and 10 in the audience. There is cheering. The speaker concludes, "We shall expose you all," and raises a clenched fist.

At this point a man who describes himself as an artist whose work could not be shown in his own country takes the microphone. "We have in this society a ruling group of bureaucrats. I denounce you all and the power you have usurped, the power of feudal lords and kings and czars. We must take the homes from the bureaucracy and give these palaces to the several million orphans in our country. The Central Committee is composed of thieves."

The artist faces Yeltsin, walks over to him, and says, "Comrade Yeltsin, I am critical of you too, but I support you against the feudal lords even though you are not really for their complete removal." He now turns to the audience, gives a clenched fist salute, and declaims, "Down with all the feudal lords. Remove them from our national life."

This is too much for rows 8, 9, and 10. In unison they stand up and attempt a hasty exit from the hall to wild applause, foot stamping, and cheers from the audience. A look of amazement crosses the face of Boris Yeltsin.

The chairperson seeks now to gain control of the meeting. He proposes to the audience a series of votes on the sense of the meeting. "In the U.S.S.R.," he states, "candidates for the position of deputy to Congress should be obliged to carry out a 'nekaz' [mandate]. Voters should impose specific duties which candidates perform. Such duties should be decided upon at meetings such as ours tonight.

"I propose that we demand of candidates that they call for a referendum on the government. Everyone in favor of demanding a referendum on the government, raise your hands in support."

As the entire hall is covered in raised hands, the chairperson continues his proposed demands: "Deputies must ensure that all people receive decent housing—flats, apartments that are adequate for their needs. Deputies must devote at least 15 percent of all profit from alcohol to building houses of culture for the youth. Deputies must support laws permitting freedom to the mass media to discuss any subject."

The hall rings with cheers of support. The chair now calls for hands in support of laws defending the rights of all citizens, not only against individual officials or functionaries but from abuse by state or collective institutions. There is unanimous support. The chair next proposes that laws should be passed permitting individual citizens to sue any functionary and governmental institutions as well. The audience responds with full support.

Yeltsin now takes the microphone and begins speaking at once, more confidently and in radical tones decidedly different from the tenor and hesitancy of his earlier remarks:

"Ours is a fight not for words but to engage in action against the bureaucratic enemy of the Soviet people. It is not just a fight for democracy but against an entrenched bureaucracy still very powerful. We have been too long traveling over roads not made by us. At long last we have reached a rupture, a break, a new direction. There can be no turning back."

The Soviet people swept Boris Yeltsin to victory with a majority of nearly 90 percent of the votes cast. It was a generalized repudiation of the party apparatus, of the ruling order. Even, as in Leningrad, where one candidate was on the ballot, voters defeated them by crossing out their names.

Boris Yeltsin is riding the tide of their discontent and is powered for now by their passion for change. But both he and his bureaucratic opponents are increasingly aware that they have very little time in which to meet the needs, expectations, and determination of the mass of Soviet working people who "will never go back again."

Back in the U.S.S.R.

By SUSAN WEISSMAN

I recently went to Moscow as part of a delegation representing the families of Leon Trotsky and Victor Serge. Trotsky's grandson Vsevolod Volkov did not accompany us, but Victor Serge's son Vlady Kibalchich, himself a victim of Stalinist repression, was part of the delegation. We carried a letter from Trotsky's grandchild and great-grandchildren to the Soviet leadership calling for the exoneration of Leon Trotsky and the publication of his works in the Soviet Union. We also carried the petition of the Moscow Trials Campaign Committee. My specific purpose on this trip was to continue the search for four manuscripts written by Serge and confiscated by the GPU upon his expulsion from the U.S.S.R. in 1936.[1] We were fortunate to be in Moscow during the election campaign and to participate in the pre-founding Congress of the Narodny Front.

Three years ago our trip would have been inconceivable. Four Americans and one Soviet/Mexican traveling to Moscow, with enormously heavy suitcases laden with Russian copies of the *Bulletin of the Left Opposition*, Trotsky's writings, Serge's *Memoirs* and novels, the journals *Critique, Against the Current, Across Frontiers,* and *Socialist Action,* not to mention a letter from actual members of Trotsky's family—not only bringing this literature to the Soviet Union, but running around openly talking about rehabilitating Serge, and that "arch-demon and lubricious viper, agent of the Okhrana, Japanese imperialism, and the Gestapo"—Leon Trotsky! We wouldn't have been able to get the literature in, and people would have run from us at the mention of our mission.

Instead we found mostly open doors and avid interest, from the intellectual, official-political, and activist communities, and from major *glasnost*-flagship press organs such as *Moscow News* and *Komsomolskaya Pravda*. So what has changed in the U.S.S.R. to have allowed seasoned supporters of the Left Opposition—routed from the Bolshevik Party in 1927 and rounded up and murdered in the years 1928-1939—to once again bring up these forbidden words and ideas? To petition for the

---

Susan Weissman is a journalist and Sovietologist. She is the coordinator of the KPFK Los Angeles radio program "Portraits of the U.S.S.R."

rehabilitation of Leon Trotsky and to publish his works, to rehabilitate Victor Serge and seek out the four books stolen from him by the GPU [KGB] upon his expulsion from the U.S.S.R. in 1936?

Clearly there are many changes which Gorbachev's twin programs of *glasnost* and *perestroika* have unleashed. The point is to understand them. Why is *perestroika* necessary, what does it mean in terms of global politics, and whose interests does it serve? The aims of the reforms are to introduce the market, reintegrate the Soviet Union into the world economy, and essentially "social-democratize" Soviet society. Gorbachev is gambling that he can keep control of a process that brings many of the contradictions of Soviet history and economic development out into the open political arena. What needs to be shown is how the current group in power in the Soviet Union is re-examining and reclaiming the forbidden history of the '20s and '30s to suit their needs: to entirely discredit the Stalinist system which has not been successful in maintaining control of the economic mechanism.

What are the concrete changes? Economically we found the U.S.S.R. a dismal and depressing place. The chronic lack of goods was everywhere in evidence, expressed in empty shelves, long lines, a dearth of fruits and vegetables, soap, and shampoo. Less essential items like batteries, film, and cassette tapes were next to impossible to find and in great demand. Living quarters were cramped and dreary.

Little in the economic sense has changed since Gorbachev came to power, except perhaps for the worse. Yet other changes are visible and real: changes in foreign policy, in the abolition of censorship, changes which allow more freedom of association and expression, and changes in the mood of both the intelligentsia and the working class.

The recent stunning election campaigns proved to be an excellent barometer of public sentiment. The town hall meetings and spontaneous demonstrations gave people an opportunity to voice their absolute intolerance for the bureaucratic apparatchiks who are seen as unaccountable opportunists with undeserved privileges. This intolerance was reflected in the ballot box as millions of Soviet voters crossed out the names of candidates associated with the status quo. As the election fervor begins to subside, however, we find that we know more about what Soviet voters are against, rather than what they are for. What is needed is a hard look at what is being proposed, in whose interests, and benefitting which social sectors, and what it all means for the Soviet working class.

The movement for reform has appeared in response to deep structural problems in Soviet society, problems which both point to the need for change and stand in the way of change. The "pre-crisis" situation Gorbachev described at the 27th Party Congress is not simply an economic crisis, but also social, political, and national as well. The economic crisis is manifest in declining and even negative growth rates, in the decline of life expectancy, which went down to 62.4 by 1984 and has since risen to 65 in 1986; and in the apparent solutions, which consist of direct pressure on the workers through the introduction of the market, and a controlled de-Stalinization. The pressure on the workers so far remains at the level of constant exhortations to work harder and various experiments to raise productivity. To make the market compatible and even integral to the Soviet model of socialism, key economists and intellectuals such as Shmelyov, Popov, and others are busy revising traditional concepts of socialism to include the morality of profit and the immorality of egalitarianism, euphemistically called "leveling."

The immediate cause of the crisis stems from the inability of the regime to control labor, and the end of the labor surplus. Workers can no longer be drawn from the countryside and the home (women) to make up for inefficiency and waste, leaving no alternative but to tackle the inefficiency itself. The solutions sought are the traditional ones of unemployment and austerity, through the introduction of the market to discipline the work force. The Soviet Union is at a crossroads, and choices are being made as to the direction ahead. In the meantime, the elite is buying time for itself by introducing a democratization process which gives more the appearance than the reality of democracy. So far the economic reforms have resulted in a stalemate, but any movement could provoke unrest on a large scale, as the regime takes on the working class.

To understand the current crisis we have to go back in history, to examine the nature of the Stalinist system established in the years 1928-41. These were the years of forced collectivization, crash industrialization, the first three five-year plans, and the purges. The significance of these events were the lasting effects they were to have on the formation of regime-worker relations. This is also the period in which the distortions of the economy began. These "distortions" are today the entrenched, permanent features of the Soviet production system which *glasnost* and *perestroika* address. The Soviets no longer equate Stalin's system with socialism, and the Stalinist system is now widely referred to as a "bureaucratically administered command economy."[2]

The Legacy of Terror

The Stalin years have become a reference point of Gorbachev's policy of *glasnost* and *perestroika* today, because long-term contradictions in

Soviet society were created by Stalin's method of rule. Stalin used terror (the purges) to systematically break resistance, undermine all sense of security in personal and social life, while concentrating political power into his own hands. At the same time he destroyed the Bolshevik Party as a Marxist political party, transforming it into an integrating agency for the elite. Thus the purges played a dual role in youthful Soviet society: that of disciplining an economically backward society in the first stages of industrialization as well as that of selecting a new economic and political elite which would organize and dominate Soviet society from that time until today. Yet the form of industrialization itself, founded on coercion with terror at its heart, created a particular form of class relations and defective production, which have reproduced themselves and become permanent features of the soviet system.

During the 1930s, policy was initiated by Stalin and executed zealously and bureaucratically by a new elite who were fearful of what could happen to them. The combination of privileges and fear cemented the loyalty of the new leading strata to Stalin. Past successes were repeated and innovation was avoided at all costs. At the base, workers had to adapt the plan's taut instructions to fit their needs. Their managers colluded with them to meet quotas in a number of ways designed to minimize the loss of workers in dreadfully short supply and to look good to their higher-ups. The tightness and extreme centralization of the plan represented an attempt to control economic events and thus the economic mechanism. But the response of the workers and managers produced the opposite effect as they lied on paper and events slipped further from the control of the center. Lying became a necessary part of the system in the atmosphere of terror.

Although the response of the workers and their managers was logical, it produced unpredictable results. The industrial structure, organized without forethought under conditions of terror, proved unworkable in practice and in need of reform to eliminate disequilibrium, disproportionality, rapid depreciation of machinery, defective construction, etc. While the society functioned at a low level of technology, simple growth was the result. Today's economy is much more complex and sophisticated, yet the problem created in the days of terror—of working with inaccurate information—makes economic calculation very difficult.

The Soviet Union in the '30s was caught in various contradictions resulting from "socialism in one country" and the emergence of a bureaucratic ruling group with Stalin at the center, who acted to maintain their power and control the system. They were compelled to run the system without going to the market, while retaining the language of socialism, which rendered official ideology useless. In order to make the system work, the resistance of the peasantry, intelligentsia, and workers had to be broken, so that mobilization and direction of labor would be met with compliance. The secret police were used to atomize the population into submission, which was accomplished through Draconian labor laws on the one hand and slave labor in the camps on the other.

But the system could not be brought under total control. The recourse to killing indicated the historical vacuum of the regime, which was neither capitalist nor socialist and had no method of known incentives or control over labor.[3] There was no threat of the reserve army of labor as under capitalism to compel productivity, nor were the workers masters of the society. The regime was left with terror as a method of control, but that brought its own problems: the killing got out of control[4] and persistent attempts to control economic events resulted in production of questionable quality except on paper.

Khrushchev attempted reforms, which represented a return to the Bukharin or Kirov solution; that is, a limited introduction of the market. The reforms of the 1960s failed, however. During the Brezhnev period, known as the time of stagnation, the system was stabilized, the standard of living rose while the economy began to decline. The ruling group became increasingly corrupt, and waste and inefficiency were the standard in the economy, as huge projects were undertaken, drawing in ever more workers. Many of the construction projects lasted decades without being completed, using old technology and obsolete materials. One of Gorbachev's first acts was to call a halt to all uncompleted projects.

During the Brezhnev years, a new social force capable of going to the market was reconstituted, the new intelligentsia that today is in favor of market reforms. At the same time, however, there still exists the successors of the old Stalinist elite who favor direct control, as well as a new working class that resists price increases and unemployment. So the situation is one of stalemate. In order to attack Stalin's heirs, Gorbachev has enlisted the help of history, and that is why the examination of the past plays such an important role in Gorbachev's attempts to reform the Soviet present.

On History and Rehabilitations

The hidden meaning of the allegorical film "Repentance" is that until Stalin is exhumed and made to stand trial for his crimes, the truth cannot emerge and the society cannot go forward. The group Memorial pushes much the same point. In other words, the reforms cannot succeed based on a false understanding of Soviet society and Soviet history. Without a knowledge of the past, the roots of the present dilemmas cannot be evaluated and without that alternatives for the future cannot be proposed.

In order to attack the group in the party apparatus that blocks his reforms, Gorbachev has resorted to attacking Stalin and rehabilitating some of Stalin's victims. This has created a dynamic which has resulted in the spectacular growth of Memorial groups across the U.S.S.R. pressing for the rehabilitation and remembrance of Stalin's victims. We attended an impressive spontaneous meeting of some 3000 people in Gorky Park on March 5, 1989, called by Memorial, one of many such meetings in Moscow. The meetings have become a focus for the many survivors and their families, who no longer wish to grieve in silence.

When Gorbachev first opened the lid on the forbidden history of the U.S.S.R., the spotlight was on the rehabilitation of Bukharin, who has become the symbol of Gorbachev's reforms, elevating him in the media to the status of anti-Stalinist hero.

Bukharin was not an anti-Stalinist, however, until he and his group faced repression. He took part in the anti-Trotsky campaign, was the originator of the concept "socialism in one country," and even in his famous speech before he was shot he protested his innocence, meaning he had always been a good Stalinist. He was in favor of the market and increased concessions to the peasantry, and that is what interests the Gorbachev group. Bukharin endorsed the one-party system, tightly controlled from the top, but liberal in the sense that NEP was liberal. In order to rehabilitate Bukharin, (February 1988) they rehabilitated everyone who was on trial with him in 1938 (the trial of the 21), which included Christian Rakovsky, one of the most famous Left Oppositionist theoreticians, whose writings are a penetrating critique of the dangers of bureaucracy and the crisis of the first five-year plan. While the rehabilitation and readmission into the party of Bukharin has meant the Soviets have published a sanitized selection of his works which suit their needs, Rakovsky's revolutionary critique has thus far not been able to get a hearing.[5]

The question of Trotsky has repeatedly come up in the Soviet Union, both in the press and society. We found a surprising receptivity to the idea of publishing his works and restoring him to his proper role in Soviet history. Most Soviet citizens are completely ignorant of Trotsky's ideas, but they are sure they don't agree with them. For the Soviet left, however, he is the real anti-Stalinist symbol. They see him as the only one of the Bolshevik Old Guard who had the political courage and personal strength to struggle against Stalinism from the very beginning till the very end.[6] He was the only one who organized political resistance to Stalin, to present a socialist alternative to Stalinism, and even in defeat, never surrendered to Stalin.

Even abroad, Trotsky, along with Victor Serge were among the tiny few who never abandoned their anti-Stalinist struggle, never abandoned Marxism, and never went over to the other side. For this reason, Boris Kagarlitsky said in an interview I conducted with him, that Trotsky is an important symbol for the left today in the U.S.S.R. and his rehabilitation would be the most significant.

The regime has had to recognize that all the Moscow Trials were rigged and the charges fabricated. Since Trotsky was painted as the main culprit for all Soviet ills, this is an implicit recognition that he was slandered. The press now admits that Trotsky was an important figure of the revolution, and the historians Yuri Afanasiev and Roy Medvedev, and the economist Otto Latsis have called for his rehabilitation, wanting to restore him to his proper place in the museum of the revolution. Articles about his grandson and his assassin have appeared in recent issues of *Moscow News;* he has been the subject of public and private meetings, newspaper and magazine articles. The purpose of the leadership is to neutralize the left, by turning Trotsky into a harmless icon, a victim whose memory should be honored and preserved.

The press has printed new distortions about Trotsky's role; the new biographer of Stalin—General Dimitri Volkogonov—has stated Trotsky opposed the revolution of 1917 along with Stalin, and when he isn't being attacked as a cosmopolitan revolutionary, read Jew, (and we were all surprised by the ferocious anti-Semitism rife in the U.S.S.R. today), he is attacked as a super-industrializer, as an arrogant authoritarian, with the implication that he would have been worse than Stalin in power. This is the way at least one section of the elite wishes to treat Trotsky. This is in stark contrast to the media treatment of Bukharin, often mentioned as Lenin's favorite. Trotsky on the other hand, the Soviet press says, was different. Lenin warned about Trotsky's "administrative approach." Administrative is a code word, synonymous with the Stalinist "bureaucratic administrative command" system.

What this means is that the regime has to revive Trotsky along with the rest of the Old Guard, though there are those in the Central Committee who are adamantly opposed to the dangerous symbolism of any Trotsky revival. Hence the new falsification of his role, to prove that Trotsky, though not a counterrevolutionary agent, was nonetheless wrong. He is thus to be cleansed of the most grotesque absurdities, while his real ideas are eviscerated. His analysis of the bureaucracy, his critique of privilege, his views of workers' democracy and genuine democratic planning in the real Marxist sense cannot be mentioned.

Some of Gorbachev's reformers appear at times to be wearing bits of Trotsky's clothes, however. There is a powerful anti-bureaucratic sentiment in the streets, which various politicians have picked up: thus Gorbachev attacks "bureaucracy" and Yeltsin criticizes privilege. Bureaucratic privilege that is, since what they want to replace it with is the legitimate privilege conferred by money.[7] But no one in the regime or the elite is proposing a revolutionary socialist solution to the problems faced by the Soviet Union today. Once again, a kernel of Trotsky's ideas are being appropriated, robbing them of their revolutionary content. In fact, one of the meetings held during Memorial's "Week of Conscience" in Moscow in November 1988 had as its theme "Stop the Second Assassination of Trotsky's Ideas."

We also attended a private meeting on Trotsky at the House of the Writers' Union, where we were introduced and Vlady, Victor Serge's son, spoke about his father and Trotsky. Apart from meeting old Bolshevik survivors, including Nadezhda Joffe, Adolf Joffe's daughter who joined the Left Opposition in 1929 and spent 27 years in camps; Aleksander Davidovich Briansky, a 106-year-old Bolshevik veteran of the revolutions of 1905 and 1917, who was with Trotsky in the Civil War; and Irina Gogua, Victor Serge's niece who survived 21 years in the cruelest camps, we found little affinity with Trotsky's ideas and many distortions of what he really represented. Yet the interest we encountered was at times enthusiastic and emotional. The Union of Writers' meeting on Trotsky greeted our delegation with a rousing ovation and were visibly delighted with Vlady's comments about his father and Trotsky. One of the speakers, the historian Stuartsev said that had Trotsky won instead of Stalin, the Soviet Union would be a better place today. The crowd divided into boos and cheers. We were told that most of the "boos" came from Pamyat supporters.

Pamyat, or Memory, is a Great Russian chauvinist, anti-Semitic group with a large following. Pamyat had members inside the Writers' Union, as well as at most of the election meetings we attended. They raised their familiar vulgar refrain of "Trotsky-zhid" (and other anti-Semitic attacks against the left today), but there, as elsewhere, we found resistance to their neo-fascist filth.

The importance of these meetings is that they demonstrate the widespread and insatiable thirst for the real truth to emerge from their hidden history. While there is little danger for the regime that the Left

Opposition will be reborn out of such meetings—the intelligentsia has more interest in the market than Marxism, and the working class is still suspicious and cynical about change—the lurking danger behind the rehabilitation of members of the Left Opposition is that theirs was the first working-class critique. The regime is moving very slowly and step by step on the rehabilitations and cosmetically publishing only what suits their purposes, consigning the rest to the museum of the revolution.

The contradiction for the regime is the clash between the need for a true understanding of social reality, which necessitates the rediscovery of the past, and the problem of how to deal within that discussion with the nature of socialism itself. For the present we have seen the new inventions of socialism, which is now against leveling (egalitarianism), for "efficiency being the only morality" (Shmelyov), who added, "we have to get rid of this perversion of an egalitarian tradition." In an interview with literary critic Alla Latynina, Shmelyov said, "I'm now thinking of patenting a new law: Every kind of inefficiency is amoral, and vice versa, everything amoral is inefficient."[8]

How will the bureaucracy deal with Trotsky's ideas when they are published? We can't know for sure, but I think they will accept with open arms his defense of the U.S.S.R. and its "planned economy," found in the *Revolution Betrayed*. For a section of the elite, Trotsky's critique of bureaucracy can be compared to their own, as well as his critique of privilege, even though his critique differs fundamentally from theirs. His anti-Stalinism is fine with them, too. By usurping Trotsky in this way they neutralize the left, undercutting potential opposition. As for Trotsky's analysis of the degenerated workers' state—well they can also agree, saying *they* are regenerating it by abolishing official privilege (and replacing it with differentials in wages based on the market). This could be the social democratization of Trotskyism.

Perestroika—and What to Do with Labor?[9]

In the fifth year of Gorbachev's *perestroika*, the lack of any economic progress is now publicly decried, and the critics say it can no longer be blamed on the "era of stagnation." Economic reform is still a slogan. The leadership appears to be floundering without clear direction. This is not simply an intellectual paralysis. There are more social scientists per capita in the Soviet Union than in any other country in the world, and judging by the press, they seem to know where they are going, but not how to get there. Articles in the newspapers call for measures to introduce the market, but progress is stymied. There is no blueprint that tells the leadership how to get to the market without meeting the working class head on.

This apparent paralysis is itself a reflection of the crisis of Soviet society, an economic crisis, a crisis which is generalized and grips all spheres of life. The fact is that *perestroika* has changed nothing in the Soviet economy despite all the talk and slogans. The popular perception is that the economic situation has deteriorated in the last three years: a public opinion poll published in *Literaturnaya Gazeta* in September 1988 reported that 72 percent of respondents felt there has been a sharp increase in prices. Long queues are very much a fact of life in the U.S.S.R. Sugar is to be rationed in Moscow and basic foodstuffs are already rationed outside the major centers. Thanks to *glasnost* there is more information about the economic situation,[10] but not real concrete changes.

The new enterprise law is a dead letter and self-financing is a sham since compulsory state procurement exists. The new cooperatives and joint ventures run into a myriad of obstacles because the economy is still governed by the command and requisitioning system. Most enterprises have to deliver 95 percent to 100 percent of production to state bodies. Ministries include all the familiar control figures. There is no price reform, although there is price increase. This increase takes the form of inexpensive goods disappearing from the shelves, leaving only much more expensive goods to buy. Neither is there a reform of wages and salaries. Life is getting harder, not the reverse, and cosmetic democratization simply underscores the transparency of the reform measures. It is difficult to talk about real democratization at the enterprise level when the commanding heights of the economy have not been democratized and enterprise-ministry relations have remained the same.

Public opinion polls attest to the growing perception that *perestroika* still belongs to the future, and not the present.

The biggest achievement of this period of *glasnost* has been to convince workers, if they needed convincing, that the status quo can no longer be maintained. In one poll 81 percent answered yes to the need for reform, while in another television survey only 2 percent thought that there had been any successes in restructuring the economy. Hence the significance of Yeltsin's showing at the polls on March 26, 1989, and the vote of no confidence in the party-appointed bureaucrats.

There is overwhelming support for change and a growing impatience with the snail's pace of change. After Gorbachev said in a speech that we must change ourselves, another survey asked the question, "Does *perestroika* have to begin with oneself?" 20.6 percent answered "No, it doesn't have to begin with oneself," and 60.3 percent said, "No, it must begin with the leaders."[11] The working class realizes that the status quo must be changed, but they are cynical about the reform which they see as one more manifestation of the constant campaign, "work harder."

While being urged to work harder, the wages of many workers have been cut because of quality-control standards (bonuses are determined by the quantity and not the quality of production) and this has provoked resentment and in many cases strikes. The workers in Kamaz took to throwing out the quality control inspectors once their take-home packets were adversely affected by the inspectors' actions. Workers have been required to work longer hours with little or no increase in pay, and goods remain in short supply. Even an increase in pay doesn't entice workers when there is little to buy with the extra money. In fact strikes seem to be a more effective way of increasing the supply of goods, albeit temporarily. A rash of strikes over the summer prompted the July 16, 1988, issue of *Pravda* to say, "The strike fever is becoming too high a price for us to pay for *perestroika*." What other option is there?

Glasnost has aroused expectation and the promise of change, and has granted the opportunity to complain more. But the economic situation has not improved and in many cases has deteriorated, the food supply remains a problem, and with greater labor discipline, there is more to complain about.

Gorbachev faces formidable problems: The apparatus resists reform, the party conservatives around Ligachev and Gosplan are convinced that change must be introduced very cautiously. So far going slowly means nothing has changed and leads only to more shrill calls for radical market reform. As the historian-archivist Yuri Afanasiev recently said, "The point is that we have to rethink the whole concept of socialism, of egalitarianism, and what it means." The attack on egalitarianism is a frontal attack on the living standards of the working class.

Labor Crisis

The Soviet press abounds with critical articles about the present economic system. Much of the blame is assigned to the workers, who "have to change the way they work." We read that the existing system encourages parasitical dependency, workers are even called a privileged group, they are lazy, they have to be shaken out of their listlessness. Forty percent of the workforce—the unskilled—have been subsidized, they are a drag on the economy, and the prescription is always the same: radical market reform.

The reformers call for "rational prices" (price increases), a serious bankruptcy law, and unemployment.[12] While in the Soviet Union, I didn't find anyone, even on the "left" who didn't think some unemployment was necessary. There is no shortage of enthusiasts for monetarism, and Margaret Thatcher was just voted "Woman of the Year" by 200,000 Soviets in a recent Moscow public opinion poll.[13]

While there seems to be a resignation that unemployment is inevitable, the responses to my queries about price increases drew a quick negative. Artyom Artyomov, a member of a new painting cooperative, explained:

"Gorbachev has told us that we must remove subsidies and allow the market to determine prices. He said our food is cheaper than in the rest of Europe. We tried our own calculations to compare but couldn't compare prices because our ruble is non-convertible. So we compared in the only way that is meaningful to us: How many hours we have to work for a kilo of bread or a pair of shoes compared to a worker in France, Germany, England, or the United States. We found that our prices are already the most expensive, and now Gorbachev wants to remove subsidies. How will we eat?"[14]

Austerity cutbacks, the solution of the International Monetary Fund (IMF), is on the order of the day. Those who propose such solutions seem to wear rose-colored glasses and remain convinced that the "downside" of the market—mass unemployment and misery—can somehow be avoided or at least not mentioned. Party conferences call for democratization and a firm hand in implementing economic reform, with no irony intended.

Market reform, as the argument goes, is the only guarantee of democracy, economic pluralism the guarantee of political pluralism. But a firm dictatorial hand is necessary to create the basis for eventual democratization. Such contradictions characterize the reform: In order to decentralize Gorbachev centralizes power, just as "illiberal" means are proposed in the pursuit of economic liberalism. In any case, pluralism in the Soviet sense is more about the divisions within the elite on how to proceed: between attacking the working class through the market, or further concessions and a system of administrative command.

The main problem today in the Soviet Union has not changed: that is how to control the working class. The old methods of direct control were accomplished first through terror and then through atomization maintained by the ubiquitous secret police, and in the end this led to a particular relationship between the workers and the regime in which inefficiency and waste seemed to be the trade-off for a docile workforce.

This was predicated however, on an abundant supply of labor which could be recruited in order to expand production. The working class today is more educated, rooted, and in short supply with no visible new reserves to draw from, such as women and peasants. The point has been reached, in which the only way forward is to change the relationship between the workers and the elite. Doing this, however, increases the possibility of further instability and crisis, so a stalemate exists.

The way forward for what is called the radical reformers is in fact the time-worn solution of divide and rule. Sociologists, such as the well-known Tatiana Zaslavskaya[15] are busy finding divisions in the working class to work on. For example:

1) the division between male and female labor: Men in U.S.S.R. earn on average 33 percent more than women. This is not based on law, but is simply a fact. It is done on the basis of women being in occupations that are worse paid than men: i.e., doctors, teachers, light industry. In fact the experiments in reform are taking place in light industry where the majority of workers are women. Evidently the regime finds it easier to control women than to control men, at least in terms of economic experiments.

Before Gorbachev came to power there were discussions about sending women back into the home. These discussions have resumed and are reflected in the media. Even the liberal *Moscow News*[16] has had articles exalting women's role in the home as the mother of the nation's children, as a nurturer who should be able fulfill her "natural role." The most back-breaking unskilled jobs in the U.S.S.R. are performed by women, and this is being denounced in the press. There have also been articles on how women workers have emasculated or feminized men! Sending women back into the home is a rather obvious way to deal with unemployment. However, this is not likely to go very far, since the average family cannot make it on one wage.

2) The division between privileged and non-privileged regions: It is no secret that Moscow and Leningrad are privileged centers, but it would be catastrophic for the regime to take away these privileges. The existence of privileged centers also maintains a division among the working class. This is bringing headaches to Moscow, however, in the form of the resurgent national struggle.

3) The division between skilled and unskilled labor: The regime is trying to use this division in order to ally the intelligentsia and skilled labor with the regime, rewarded by higher pay. This is what the leveling campaign (against egalitarianism) is about. The way it is presented is between those workers who work hard and have "a social conscience," and

the rest who simply collect their pay while not working or working badly. Although the intelligentsia widely support this tack, the working class does not, and so the regime has had great difficulty in moving in this direction. In an article in the February 1988 *Ekonomichiskaya Gazeta* the Deputy Chairman of the State Commission on Labor discussed the failure thus far in overcoming "egalitarianism in the payment of labor."

What this shows is that the regime is unwilling to introduce the measures it needs for its own program because it means it will have to take on the working class. This is a qualitative difference from the past, when workers were openly repressed and strikers were punished with execution, even in the 1960s. The shortage of labor, the increased weight of the working class, and the need for a skilled workforce that has a stake in the system all militate against the use of repression. Hence, the regime is in a bind and is seeking even short-term solutions.

One such solution would be to resolve the problem of agriculture. Food is a crucial question in the U.S.S.R., and any improvement in the food supply could raise the standard of living. Agriculture is the one area in the Soviet economy where privatization can succeed, at least in the short term.

They are likely to have some success in small-group agriculture that is labor-intensive, such as vegetable gardening. Wheat production would be more difficult to privatize because the real problem in agriculture is industry; the farms need machinery that doesn't break down constantly, pesticides and fertilizers, proper irrigation and drainage, storage and transport, and roads to deliver their products—all of which are dependent on industry working. In order to have better agriculture (food), industry must be efficient, and in order to do that they have to deal with incentives or a higher standard of living—so it is a vicious circle. The situation cannot change until industry is changed, and since they cannot change industry without taking on the working class, agriculture in the long term cannot be changed.

So to return to the question, can the policy of market reform succeed? Certainly not without provoking serious social unrest. The regime has withheld introducing price increases, a cornerstone of their market reforms, for they are afraid of galvanizing a situation similar to what occurred in Novocherkassk in 1962, where strikes, factory occupations and riots spread rapidly in response to price increases on meat and dairy products and were put down by the army, leaving hundreds dead. Is there an alternative?

The working class sees no alternative. They know they don't have socialism, and the regime now openly says it. There is no obvious alternative on the horizon. That does not mean the working class is politically confused, but simply that they cannot see where to go. The working class is not socialist or Marxist, and rejects the status quo: It appears they don't want another awful regime, and they have to be convinced that an alternative can come about.

The Soviet working class is strong in relation to its recent past. It is an industrialized and socialized working class assembled in huge factories that are relatively concentrated in certain areas of the U.S.S.R.: It would be a difficult working class to contain. The problem Gorbachev faces is what forms to use to control this formidable obstacle: either the form of control under capitalism—unemployment—or some other form. Historically in the Soviet Union, the form they have used has been direct force, and later the KGB. The problem for the regime is that they can no longer use direct force in the same way. It is economically inefficient. The regime can no longer afford unproductive measures, and brute force is also ruled out, so we see the increasing power of the working class.

What Alternatives?

Do the liberal intelligentsia and the new left offer an alternative for the working class? They are caught up in the debate on market reform and democratization. We didn't meet anyone in the U.S.S.R. who was opposed to the introduction of the market. The difference between the liberal elite and the new left is that the latter seem to believe that the market can be introduced without attacking the living standards of the working class. Many of the so-called liberals are openly monetarist, calling for unemployment and making workers "fight for the right to work."[17]

The real question for leftists is not over whether or not there is a role for market elements in the economy—this is a secondary issue. The question evades the fundamental issue which is social and political: In whose interests is the society organized and how can the transformation of social relations be achieved? Can a thoroughgoing and authentic democratization of Soviet society be accomplished from above?

The current reform documents do not address the question of accountability nor democratization of economic management at all levels, beginning at the center. So long as the ministries remain the same and central authorities are not subject to democratic control, the reform is at best partial and cosmetic. Democratization is not merely an external condition to facilitate the carrying out of economic reform; democracy is the essence of reform.[18] But real democracy can only result from below, from the working class taking the superficial democratic reform measures and translating them into genuine democratic control. This is precisely what scares the reformers.

In the meantime what we do see is a very important growth and revitalization of public opinion. This has been demonstrated in the spectacular growth of informal organizations in the past two years, the keen participation in the election process, the seemingly insatiable thirst for knowledge about the Soviet past and the present, reflected in soaring magazine subscriptions, spontaneous meetings and rallies, and constant discussions. Ludmila Alexeyeva has estimated that some 3 million people now participate in more than 30,000 informal groups, with 300,000 discussing directly political questions.

There are informal organizations corresponding to a variety of interests, including right-wing chauvinist and neo-fascist groups, such as Pamyat (Memory) and Otyechestvo (Fatherland). The question of nationalism has mobilized millions of people in the republics, acting as a focus for social tension. An increasingly popular economic slogan has been raised in the Baltic republics, which finds an echo elsewhere—economic sovereignty. In the present economic situation this appears to be a possible alternative.

The informal groups are in constant flux, regrouping and reforming. Workers groups are forming and discussing self-management and the formation of independent trade unions. While the formation and growth of workers' groups is a significant development, the informal organizations are still principally made up of discontented intellectuals, teachers, students, and engineers. We found no organizations which stand on the working class alone.

The New Soviet Left

The Soviet dissidents of the early 1970s were effectively dispersed by repression and emigration. The end of the '70s and early '80s saw the birth of a new socialist opposition, around the journals "Left Turn," "Alternatives," and "Searches." The new leftists were young intellectuals acquainted with the Western new left tradition who wished to marry market reforms and the plan. Reading pro-market economists such as Vladimir Brus and Alec Nove, they hoped the market would loosen up society to allow political organization, and to act as an indicator of consumer needs and a check on the quality of goods.

Repressed and broken up in the last years of Brezhnev, freed by Andropov, this current has re-emerged today and is behind the birth of the

Federation of Socialist Clubs (August 1987), which split in the summer of 1988, giving rise to the constellation of groups we spent the most time with in Moscow, called the Narodny or (Moscow) People's Front. Its most visible member is Boris Kagarlitsky, known in the West mainly through *New Left Review*, and the recent recipient of the Isaac Deutscher prize for his book *The Thinking Reed*.

The Narodny Front in Moscow is made up of some 34 organizations, ranging from the chauvinist, anti-Semitic "All-Russian Democratic Union" led by Stanislav Dergunov to the democratic Thatcherites of the "Democratic Union"[19] in the so-called center to ecologists, anarchists, and the left in the "Club of Socialist Initiatives," whose leading activists are Boris Kagarlitsky and Mikhail Maliutin. The slogans of the Narodny Front are "democracy, socialism, ecology."

The New Left has reproduced much of the political spectrum we are familiar with in the West. There are Bakuninists who are also sympathetic to Trotsky in the group "Obshchina" or "Commune," Gramscianos, those intrigued with the Frankfurt School, Latin-Americanists in the Che Guevara Club, ecologists and eco-feminists, social democrats in Democratic Perestroika—and we even met young historians who called themselves Left SRs.[20]

On March 10-11, 1989, we attended the pre-founding Congress of the People's Front, the new regroupment of FSOK. They successfully fielded a candidate, the historian Sergei Stankevich, in the recent national elections for the Soviet Congress, and have grown enormously in size and influence.[21] Many of their members are also CPSU members (Stankevich, for example) who belong to the "renewal" faction within the party. The Front supported Yeltsin in the current election process. In an interview with Kagarlitsky, I questioned their support for Yeltsin, who represents a more rapid and thorough application of market reform, which is based on an attack on the living standards of the working class. Kagarlitsky agreed but countered that Yeltsin has the support of the working class, was ousted for being a "radical," and moreover, he is rhetorically very aggressive on the themes of social justice and privilege, which resonate deeply in the Soviet working class. Kagarlitsky likened their support for Yeltsin, who is a functionary, albeit a radical one, to the way leftists in the United States support "progressive" Democrats. Yeltsin as the Soviet Jesse Jackson?

The Narodny Front is contradictory: They are in favor of socialist pluralism, self-management of production, and the democratization of planning, the abolition of censorship, no attacks on the working class. They are in favor of a mixed economy, using the market as I already mentioned along with democratic planning. To ease the pain of bankruptcy and factory closures, they want retraining schemes organized and resettlement compensation as well as unemployment insurance. They are anti-dogmatic, which I found very refreshing, but have inherited many of the bureaucratic habits of their society,[22] and seem too taken with the opium of the market and social democratic solutions.

They are a product of their own history and society and have much to share with Western leftists, as well as a debt to pay: Kagarlitsky said that he and his comrades feel a particular burden and duty to the international left—they are part of a history and tradition which produced Stalinism, distorted Marxism, and discredited the socialist idea. Thus they felt it incumbent upon them now to cleanse the concept of socialism of its Stalinist stains and rescue socialism for the international struggle.

The situation I have described is one of stalemate resulting from the inability of the regime to impose austerity on the working class, and of an economy in decline and in need of reform. What develops in the course of the attempts at implementation of the reforms is the big question. We do know that without reform there will be further decline. If the reforms are implemented we can expect to see a polarization of Soviet society and big struggles. Either way, the future depends on the actions of the working class. Perhaps the prophecy of a repressed revolutionary who perished in Stalin's gulag will come to pass. In June 1930 he wrote Victor Serge: " . . . we shall serve as manure to fertilize the earth in which after us new human harvests of the revolution will spring up."

NOTES

1. See *Against the Current* No. 12-13, p. 45. I did not return with the manuscripts, nor had I expected to find them so easily, but was able to generate interest in Victor Serge, whose revolutionary novel of the purges, *The Case of Comrade Tulayev,* was just serialized in the provincial literary journal *Ural,* and to trace the history of the stolen manuscripts with a little more precision. The campaign continues.
2. This formulation is now commonplace in the Soviet press.
3. H.H. Ticktin, "The Political Economy of the Purges," Paper delivered to the American Association for the Advancement of Slavic Studies, Boston, November 1987.
4. Estimates of the numbers killed vary widely, both in the West and

the Soviet Union, where the subject has been passionately taken up by the Memorial movement. One sociologist estimates that up to 50 million were killed by Stalin in the course of collectivization, famine, and purges. See Dr. Igor Bestuzhev-Lada in *Nedelya*, February 1988, and Anton Antonov-Ovseyenko in his *The Time of Stalin*. Although the estimates are still estimates and not "counts," what is interesting is that now that the Soviets are looking into the issue, they are coming up with numbers far higher than ever estimated in the West, even by hard-line cold warriors.

5. There are people who are trying to get Rakovsky's famous letter to Valentinov published ("On the Professional Dangers of Power").
6. Interview with Kagarlitsky, *Critique* 22.
7. Yeltsin interview, *Pravda*, conducted by Pavel Voshchanov, *Komsomolskaya Pravda*, Dec. 31, 1988, p. 4.
8. *Moscovsky Novosti*, No. 10, March 13-20, 1988, p. 11.
9. Some of the background information and insights for this section came from a round table Hillel Ticktin, Bohdan Krawchenko, Michael Cox, and myself participated in at the annual Slavic association conference in Hawaii in November 1988.
10. For example, the national debt is now admitted, and calculated to be around 570 billion rubles. See *Moscow News* No. 18, May 7-14, 1989, p. 10.
11. L. Kostin, "Otchuzhdenie," *Sotsiologicheskiye issledovania*, No. 2, 1988.
12. For example, V. Seliunin said that 25 percent, or one-fourth, of the work force in industry could be eliminated, and Nikolai Shmelyov wrote "at least 20 percent to 25 percent of the work force employed in industry today is superfluous to the production process even according to our technical terms." "Ekonomika i zdravyi smysl," (Economics and Common Sense) by Nikolai Shmelyov in *Znamia*, July 1988, 179-184. The issue contains a discussion on *perestroika* proposals by economists V. Seliunin, N. Shmelyov, Gabriel Popov, and Otto Latsis.
13. *Moscow News* weekly No. 15, 1989, p. 6.
14. From an interview I conducted in Moscow, March 8, 1989.
15. Academician Zaslavskaya, President of the Soviet sociological Association, told Ye. Manucharova in an interview which appeared in *Izvestia*, April 21, 1987, p. 3, that the old "deliberately oversimplified formula—'two classes and one stratum' . . . does not correspond to the real structure of our society." Instead, Zaslavskaya says that her "deep conviction" is that Soviet society is made up of

"dozens, if not hundreds, of groups and strata whose statuses in society and the national economy differ substantially." She further says "each group has its own interests" and that the "conflict of groups with differing interests" is necessary for the realization of restructuring.
16. See the special articles on women in the March 1988 issues around International Women's Day.
17. Zaslavskaya, *op.cit.*
18. Bohdan Krawchenko, Roundtable discussion on *perestroika*, Slavic Association annual conference, November 1988.
19. Within Democratic Union itself there is a range from pluralist monetarists to social democrats.
20. The Left Socialist Revolutionaries participated in the October Revolution and supported the Bolsheviks until the Peace of Brest-Litovsk.
21. For example, in Cheriomuzhinski district, where Stankevich ran, the Narodny Front increased their size ten fold.
22. For example, they spent 75 percent of the first day of their two-day pre-founding Congress to elect the Presidium for the Congress.

Moscow News Interviews Touring U.S. Trotskyists

*The following article appeared on page 12 of **Moskovskiya Novosti** (MN) issue No. 13, dated March 26, 1989.*

*MN has been in the forefront of the campaign for more openness, or **glasnost**, and has become known for offering more open discussions on more issues than most Soviet periodicals. Printed in a run of approximately 250,000 Russian-language copies in the U.S.S.R., MN also appears abroad, published in translation into a number of foreign languages.*

*Contrary to the normal practice, this article was excluded from the English-language publication, **Moscow News**. In what could not have been an accident, the corresponding space on page 12 of the English-language paper carried an article entitled "Why Siberian **Pravda** Criticizes MN," the opening sentence of which reads: "The newspaper **Pravda** differs, depending on where you read it."*

*This is what should have been in that space. We are indebted to Trotsky bibliographer Louis Sinclair for bringing this article to our attention.—**Marilyn Vogt-Downey** (Co-chair, U.S. Moscow Trials Campaign Committee)*

Request for Rehabilitation

American Delegation Delivers to Moscow a Petition From the Descendents of Trotsky

"We, the undersigned, the grandson and great-grandchildren of the Russian revolutionary Marxist Lev Davidovich Bronstein, known as Lev [Leon] Trotsky . . . request that all the slander and false criminal charges raised against him on the direct orders of Stalin be officially withdrawn from our grandfather and great-grandfather, his family, and his comrades in struggle. . . .

"We also request that the works of Leon Trotsky, which represent a valuable collection of historic and contemporary Marxist study and thought be freely published in the Soviet Union."

The letter with this petition, signed by direct descendents of Trotsky who live in Mexico, was brought to Moscow by four members of the "Moscow Trials Committee" in the U.S.A., which is studying the crimes of Stalinism. Joining them was Vladimir Kibalchich, the son of Victor Serge, a Russian revolutionary well known in the West, who was repressed by Stalin for participating in the "Left Opposition."

"In recent months, a whole number of well-known party activists repressed under Stalin have been restored to a place of honor," said Carl Finamore, a journalist from the radical American newspaper *Socialist Action*. "It seems to us that the time has come to do the same with respect to Trotsky, regardless of what one may think of his political views. All that is necessary is to affirm, for example, that the charge made against him that he conspired to murder the top Soviet leaders was a lie."

"Every person must have the opportunity independently to judge Trotsky's views, after having read his works—and they comprise 80 volumes—and to become familiar with precisely what he meant by 'permanent revolution.' As it is now, people in the Soviet Union to a significant degree are still under the influence of the view of Trotsky that was formulated by Stalin himself," was the opinion of social activist and the director of the "Campaign in Support of Palestine," Ralph Schoenman.

Members of the American group sought a meeting with Trotsky's granddaughter Aleksandra of Moscow; however, they learned that she had died literally on the eve of their arrival.—**Andrei Bezruchenko**

PART FOUR

The Struggle of the Oppressed Nationalities

Introduction to Nationalist Struggle in the U.S.S.R.

By NAT WEINSTEIN

The following brief review should be useful to the reader, who may be unfamiliar with the revolutionary Marxist view of nationalism, for understanding the complex role of this phenomenon in today's world.

Is nationalism progressive or reactionary? This is one of the questions most misunderstood by serious fighters for human rights. The confusion is largely due to the way the question is posed.

All nationalisms cannot be placed under the same heading. Serious people must ask *which* nationalism is being considered—that of the oppressor or that of the oppressed? Three graphic examples of diametrically opposed nationalisms immediately come to mind: The nationalism of white America versus the nationalism of Black America, that of white South Africa versus that of Black South Africa, and the nationalism of Jewish Zionism versus that of the Arabs in Palestine.

In each case, the nationalism of the one is opposed to the nationalism of the other. In each case, a whole people—irrespective of social class—is denied a greater or lesser portion of the natural rights owed all human beings residing in the given geographical area.

For this simple reason alone, the nationalism of the exploiters and oppressors in America, South Africa, and Palestine—of all those who deny subjugated nations, nationalities, or racial groups their natural rights—is reactionary; while the nationalism of those denied their natural rights in these three places is progressive.

This is a good beginning guideline for determining the objective character of the many expressions of nationalism in the world today and throughout history.

In each of the cases so far considered, opposing national interests cannot be understood apart from the class struggle. Nationalism is set into motion and is conditioned by the opposing interests of the two main classes in modern society—workers and capitalists.

Nat Weinstein is Co-National Secretary of Socialist Action.

The question of nationalism must be set in the context of the Marxist principle of proletarian internationalism: The class interests of the workers in all countries transcend the boundaries of nationality. An advance or retreat by workers in one country accordingly strengthens or weakens workers everywhere else. And the logic of the struggle for freedom of the world's workers is toward the abolition of all national boundaries in a global socialist confederation.

Workers of any dominant national grouping have absolutely nothing to gain from the super-exploitation of their counterparts among the oppressed nationalities. While they may have a *relatively* privileged position *vis-a-vis* their oppressed class sisters and brothers, they are also exploited and oppressed, albeit to a lesser degree.

The relative privileges of the workers in the dominant nationality, however, tend to create in their minds the illusion that they are *beneficiaries* of the system of inequality and that they have a vested interest in perpetuating national or racial oppression.

On the contrary, the system under which workers of oppressed nationalities are generally denied such things as equal pay and equal access to jobs works to *depress* the living standards of the "privileged" workers. The lowered living standards of the oppressed workers aggravate competition between workers. Class solidarity, a strategic requirement for an effective struggle to advance the living standards of all workers, is thus undermined.

The illusion is carefully and systematically cultivated by the true beneficiaries of national oppression, the capitalist class. The labor bureaucracies and other reformists are among the chief instruments of the capitalists for sowing and perpetuating this reactionary illusion.

This privileged parasitic layer encrusted on the economic and political institutions created by the working class has tied its caste interests to those of the ruling capitalist class, and thus indirectly benefits from the oppression of national and racial groups.

Union bureaucrats in the United States, for example, gravitate toward the most backward sections of the working class to secure a base for their class-collaborationist policies. They more or less openly cater to the racist attitudes capitalism inculcates within the ranks of society in general and the working class in particular. This more-or-less subtle identification by labor's misleaders with national and racial oppression creates a much bigger problem for the revolutionary workers' movement than meets the eye.

The division thus created between Black and white workers, for example, often becomes so acute as to be unbridgeable by routine sloganizing for working-class "unity." That's why, for example, it is correct to support a range of demands—including separatist demands—arising from the Black freedom movement seeking immediate redress for centuries of racial injustice.

It will be extremely difficult, if not impossible, for the working-class movement in the United States to achieve the highest levels of solidarity without the clearest demonstrations of support for Black demands ranging from affirmative action to the unqualified right to *independent* Black economic, political, and social organization and action.

At this point in history, this is the only sure road to working-class solidarity—without which effective defense of its class interests, not to mention the conquest of working-class political power, is impossible.

The Soviet Union has been likened by the revolutionary Marxist movement to a trade union that has taken state power and rules in the historic interests of the world working class. But it is viewed as a union that has degenerated under the misleadership of a bureaucratic caste which has conquered political power by the most ruthless terroristic gangster methods such as we have seen on a relatively small scale in American unions.

The Bolshevik Party of Lenin and Trotsky, which led the workers of Czarist Russia to victory, had the clearest understanding of how national divisions within the working class can and must be overcome.

On the one hand, the workers' councils (soviets) that constituted the government of the revolutionary state created by the October Revolution were unambiguously committed to full equality for all national components of the Soviet Republic. Where Czarist Russia, with the support of the capitalists from the dominant regions, skillfully played one nationality against another, the workers' government worked assiduously to overcome national divisions.

The democratic soviet power took note of the residual effects of Czarist Imperial Russia, which had earned it the designation of "prisonhouse of nations." This history made it difficult to erase the legacy of chauvinist indoctrination of many workers belonging to dominant nationalities in their areas, especially in Russia.

The fears and suspicion of the long-oppressed nationalities could not be wiped out in a single stroke. Lenin and Trotsky tirelessly explained that the unity of the Soviet workers' state could only be gained if the constituent nationalities had the right to self-determination—including the right to separation.

In 1922 this right was institutionalized, and the Union of Soviet Socialist Republics was established as a voluntary association of autonomous republics with the right to form independent Soviet socialist republics.

Stalin, however, quickly embarked on a course that negated the internationalist conquests of the Bolshevik Party and the Soviet state. As early as 1923, Stalin engineered the bureaucratic repression of Georgian Bolsheviks who sought to defend the national interests of their people against bureaucratic abuse.

Lenin, in response, proposed a bloc with Trotsky against this violation of Bolshevik principles. Following Lenin's death in January 1924, and with the consolidation of Stalin's power, the right to autonomy and self-determination became an empty juridical "guarantee" that existed on paper but was systematically violated in everyday life.

Today we are witnessing a desperate attempt by Mikhail Gorbachev, the undisputed representative of the essentially unreconstructed Stalinist bureaucracy, to preserve the dictatorship of the ruling caste.

Gorbachev's *glasnost* (openness) is not the beginning of the self-reform of bureaucratic totalitarianism, but rather a tactical retreat. It is no accident that Gorbachev's "reform" of the Soviet constitution includes abolition of the nominal autonomy of the associated republics. This act, alone, gives the lie to his alleged goal of truly democratizing the Soviet Union.

The articles in this section, which focus on the progressive character of the nationalist struggle, help deepen our understanding of the *revolutionary* nationalism of oppressed peoples.

Gorbachev Faces Deep Crisis in the Baltic States

By HAYDEN PERRY

The wave of regional nationalism that is rolling across the Soviet Union has reached the shores of the Baltic. The people of Latvia, Estonia, and Lithuania are in the streets demanding the restoration of their national languages, their cultures, and their national identities.

In an unprecedented move, the Estonian Supreme Soviet passed a constitutional amendment requiring Estonian approval of any Soviet law applied to them. The Estonians also issued a "declaration of sovereignty," asserting Estonia's independence in all areas except defense and foreign affairs. They also want the text of the Hitler-Stalin pact of 1939 published to expose the truth about their forcible annexation by the Soviet Union.

Hitler invited Stalin to take over these three small nations as part of the deal that divided Poland and gave Hitler the green light for his war of conquest. The Baltic people were not consulted as their nations were obliterated.

Latvia, Estonia, and Lithuania had been independent nations for 22 years—from 1917 to 1939. For centuries they had been ruled by Germans, Swedes or Russians.

When Stalin took over the Baltic states, he integrated their economies into the socialized property relations of the Soviet Union. Despite the bureaucratic, dictatorial way this was accomplished, there is little evidence the Baltic people preferred the rule of the former capitalists and landlords.

However, the Baltic peoples did resist when Stalin resumed the policy the Czars had pursued in vain: to Russianize these states and turn them into provinces where Russian culture predominated, with the economies controlled in the interests of Moscow. Thousands of Baltic people were deported to Siberia by Stalin. Thousands of Russians were sent to the Baltic states to replace them. Large factories were built, without regard to local needs, to employ the newcomers.

Hayden Perry is a staffwriter for **Socialist Action** *newspaper.*

Minority in Their Own Land

In Estonia only 60 percent of the population is now Estonian. In Latvia the native population is a minority in its own land. Instead of the Russian settlers learning Latvian, the Latvians have to learn Russian. "For over 40 years I have watched the culture and economy of my country slowly deteriorate," said a Latvian quoted in *The New York Times*.

Now the Latvians have organized to fight back. They have formed the Latvian Popular Front, with a membership of over 100,000. They demand complete economic independence, the right to create their own currency, to establish independent relations with other states, and the right to control travel and immigration.

In Lithuania a new movement, "Lithuanians in Support of Perestroika," held a congress in October that voiced nationalist demands, including the right to their own language and national flag. These demands are backed by the vast majority of the Lithuanians, as attested by a petition campaign that gathered 1.5 million signatures out of a population of 3.6 million.

Under Stalin, raising such demands would result in a fast trip to Siberia, or worse. But today, the political and economic crisis of the bureaucracy that gave rise to Gorbachev's *glasnost* policy has created a wide channel for expressing grievances against national oppression. However, the intensity of nationalist feeling expressed has taken the Kremlin by surprise.

Demonstrations of 300,000 make the unrest obvious. Local Communist Party officials have joined the Popular Front and are supporting their demands. This reflects the broad base of support this movement has, but also the unwillingness of the Kremlin to confront the nationalist movement head on, at this time.

Riding Out the Storm

The ongoing crisis in Soviet Armenia and the unrest in the Ukraine indicate that nationalism is a major threat to the stability of Gorbachev's regime. The history of the Baltic republics as recently independent nations makes the situation there particularly volatile. Communist Party leaders in the Baltic states, in most cases, have joined the nationalists, only to counsel patience.

The Kremlin has yielded to some demands, permitting the display of national flags, and tolerating the new national movements. But the bureaucrats want to keep the movement within limits they can control.

A serious limit was set when Gorbachev proposed deleting the right of a republic to secede from the Soviet federation. This right has been a basic policy since the founding of the first workers' state. Even Stalin did not remove this fundamental socialist right from his 1936 Constitution. Exercising this right, of course, would be another matter.

Deleting this right has created alarm among the Baltic people. This was intensified as they learned of other changes to be proposed at the coming Presidium of the Supreme Soviet. The Estonians hear the Supreme Soviet will tighten, rather than loosen, Moscow's control of these states.

They challenged Gorbachev by calling for an Estonian veto of Soviet laws that impact badly on Estonia. The Estonians were careful to say these measures would not be a call to secede from the Soviet Union. Their demand, they stated, was for genuine equality among Soviet republics. Popular Front spokesman Edgar Savisaar, who is also a Communist Party member, said "We want a sovereign Estonia inside the Soviet Union."

Gorbachev has responded to the Estonian challenge with a call to "talk it over." He has already said some of his proposed laws could be modified. But he rejected the Estonian declaration of sovereignty as a threat to the integrity of the Soviet Union.

The people of Latvia and Lithuania are demonstrating support of Estonia, although these two republics have not issued a similar declaration of sovereignty.

There is sentiment for total independence among the Baltic people, but, even as independent states, they say, they would preserve socialized property relations, and maintain relations of equality with other Soviet republics and other workers' states.

But this development would not be acceptable to the Kremlin. Gorbachev hopes, however, by concessions that stay short of true equality among the republics, to contain the nationalist sentiments of the Baltic people.

A key factor, besides the political concessions Gorbachev is forced to grant, is the bureaucracy's inability to solve the shortages and other economic ills that are straining Soviet society to the breaking point. Scarcity of consumer goods, and the role of a privileged caste are major factors intensifying the national aspirations of the many minorities that make up the Soviet Union.

Gorbachev Uses Earthquake to Attack Armenians

By GERRY FOLEY

On Dec. 12, 1988, *Pravda,* the newspaper of the Communist Party of the Soviet Union (CPSU), admitted facts that showed that while the recent Armenian earthquake was a natural occurrence, the scale of damage and loss of life was in fact caused by the mismanagement of the economy during the "years of stagnation." This was a direct reference to the period under Leonid Brezhnev.

"Everything that was built during those years of stagnation collapsed," the *Pravda* article noted. "How could it be otherwise, since seismologists warned the builders several times. . . . Nevertheless, buildings of five, eight floors rose up stubbornly."

The construction of the housing projects was of poor quality. Buildings that had "more sand than cement"—to quote *Pravda*— collapsed like a house of cards with the first tremor.

The attempt to blame shoddy construction on Brezhnev is not likely to convince the Armenian masses. This sort of construction is typical of the bureaucracy's economic mismanagement everywhere from the time the bureaucratic caste usurped political power and freed itself from democratic control.

"When the earthquake left 100,000 victims buried in ruins, when the Armenians were plunged into sorrow, and hundreds left the capital to help their fellow citizens, the people were stabbed in the back," the Karabakh Committee, the 11-person leadership of the Armenian independent mass movement, declared in a Dec. 11, 1988, communiqué published on Dec. 17 in the French daily *Libération:*

"No other country, even the least democratic, would have dared to insult the mourning of our people, who were beaten and wounded by bullets two days after the earthquake. In view of Moscow's attitude, it is hard to convince the people that the only problem is a natural earthquake.

"This catastrophe has served to show that we were really deprived of

---

Gerry Foley is the editor of **International Viewpoint** *magazine.*

sovereignty. . . . Gorbachev sent his army to shut down the Karabakh Committee. Then he came to offer his condolences to our people. He arrested people, he shed blood, and he left. All those who do not condemn that, condemn themselves to slavery."

The reaction of the Karabakh Committee was on the mark. The Kremlin's attack on the Armenian movement had clearly nothing to do with maintaining "order." It was a response to the Karabakh Committee's attempt to mobilize support for the victims of the earthquake in the face of the paralysis, incompetence, and confusion of the bureaucratic institutions.

Supposedly, one of the principal objectives of *perestroika* is to promote rank-and-file initiative. But who could doubt that an organization that had proved itself capable of organizing demonstrations of up to a third of the population of the Armenian Soviet Socialist Republic as well as national general strikes could effectively organize help for the earthquake victims?

Committee Leaders Arrested

During the days immediately following the earthquake—the most important days in the rescue operation—the population had to rely on its own efforts. All eyewitness accounts agree in stating that the official relief agencies responded to the emergency late and inefficiently. But the self-organization of the Armenians to rescue the victims was brutally repressed by the Soviet armed forces.

A correspondent for the French daily *Le Monde* reported on Dec. 13, 1988:

"While all the sirens were screaming and the ambulances continued to bring hundreds of wounded to the Yerevan surgical institute, on Dec. 10 the military authorities in the city forcibly dispersed a crowd that had come to offer contributions for the victims."

Five leaders of the 11 on the Karabakh Committee were arrested and sentenced to 30 days in prison after they refused to call on the people to go home. The following day, Sunday, Dec. 11, troops fired warning shots to disperse a crowd gathered to protest the arrests. Reports of the number wounded vary from one to three, but there seems no doubt that blood was shed. [See Karabakh Committee leader Raphael Khazaryan's "Open Letter to Mikhail Gorbachev" following this article.—**ed.**]

For over a year, the Soviet authorities had refrained from using violence against the independent Armenian mass movement. It was only after the latest anti-Armenian pogroms in Azerbaidjan that the authorities began to punish the victims, rather than those responsible for the violence. Now, in an open and blatant manner, the Soviet leadership decided to exploit the earthquake disaster to attempt to crush the Armenian mass movement.

The Soviet bureaucrats welcomed the hypocritical assistance of the imperialist nations—of those who at best offered only a few crumbs to the hurricane victims in Nicaragua. But at the same time, they condemned the efforts of the leaders of the Armenian people to come to the aid of their own people.

Rise of Independent Mass Activity

The Armenian people have played the vanguard role in the struggle of oppressed peoples fighting for national rights. That is undoubtedly why the Kremlin is taking the gamble of trying to crush them now.

The bureaucracy's crackdown in Armenia poses a life-or-death challenge to the movements of other oppressed peoples, but not only to them.

The movements for national rights are the first form of the revival of independent mass activity since the establishment of the bureaucratic dictatorship. They have been opening the road for democratic action by the Russian workers themselves.

The democratic aspirations of all the Soviet masses explain why the bureaucracy could not crush the movements for national rights at their birth. Therefore, the attacks being carried out on them today—in particular on the Armenian movement—represent a turnabout by the Gorbachev leadership that threatens the entire movement for democratic and social rights of every kind in the U.S.S.R.

No socialist or democrat should be confused about the terms of this confrontation by the bureaucracy's claims about the dangers of "nationalism," "communal conflict," or "local Mafia." What is at stake is the right of the masses to solve their problems through mobilization, open debate, and democracy.

Imprisoned Armenian Leader, Raphael Khazaryan, Sends "Open Letter" to Mikhail Gorbachev

On Jan. 9, 1989, Raphael Khazaryan, a renowned scientist and leader of the Karabakh Committee in Armenia, was arrested in the capital city of Yerevan together with other Armenian nationalists. A week later he was moved to Moscow, where he was detained at the Boutirki Prison.

The Struggle of the Oppressed Nationalities 159

The Karabakh Committee is the recognized leadership of the mass movement for Armenian national rights. It has been fighting to have Nagorno-Karabakh, an oppressed Armenian enclave in Azerbaidjan, returned to the Armenian Soviet Socialist Republic.

On Jan. 17-18, 1989, elections for candidates to the Supreme Soviet were held at the Physics Institute of the Academy of Sciences in Yerevan. The participants rejected the official candidate nominated by the director of the institute and instead proposed Khazaryan, the prisoner.

*On Dec. 10, 1988, following the arrest of five other Karabakh Committee members, Khazaryan wrote an "Open Letter to Mikhail Gorbachev" expressing his views on Gorbachev's **perestroika** reforms. The following are brief excerpts from this letter.*

"Bitterness, disillusionment, and the crumbling of our last hopes in the possibility of justice—such were the reactions of the Armenian people after the interview you gave the press before leaving Armenian territory. . . . [Gorbachev had lambasted the Karabakh Committee as "unscrupulous demagogues" and "parasitical rumormongers."—**ed.**]

"You say that we, the militants in the mass movements, are the obstacle to the development of *perestroika*. But do you really think you will achieve *perestroika* and democracy on the basis of your sole authority—by simply replacing the individual in the post of general secretary while at the same time preserving 90 percent of the old apparatus?

"There is no cure for the apparatus so long as the entire chain of candidates, raised in the party's incubators and impatient to rise up one more rung, is not shattered. You have legitimized this usurpation of political power by concentrating unlimited powers in your own hands. Now we must bury our hopes in democracy, for democracy is incompatible with absolutism.

"I won't hide from you the fact that I believed in you, as did many others. I hoped that I would spend the rest of my life in a society free from servitude. I rejoiced in your victories against the 'enemies of *perestroika*.' It is a bitter thing to have to shed my illusions. . . .

"Do you want to hear about the elections to the Supreme Soviet of the [Armenian] Republic, where we rejected the candidacies of the gangsters proposed by the Central Committee of the Republic?

"This rejection of the official candidates took place in spite of an entire operation mobilized from above, beginning with the party apparatus and the state security agencies all the way down to the criminal elements—in spite of the military occupation of the polling sites and the fraud (900 ballots were secretly slipped into the box). Yes, the people for the first time refused to take part in the old, humiliating comedy of 'choosing the best watermelon from a batch of one.' Despite all the intrigue, the official candidates were repudiated. . . .

"Despite the slanders, the barbarous repression, and the arrests, the people know how to separate truth from falsehood. They understand the true reasons for the crusade by the corrupt ones to defend their powers and privileges."

Background to the Struggle in the Ukraine

By ZBIGNIEW KOWALEWSKI

"The bureaucracy strangled and plundered the people within Great Russia too," Leon Trotsky wrote about the Stalinist system. "But in the Ukraine matters were further complicated by the massacre of national hopes. Nowhere did restrictions, purges, repressions, and in general all forms of bureaucratic hooliganism assume such murderous sweep as they did in the Ukraine against the powerful, deeply rooted longings of the Ukrainian masses for greater freedom and independence."[1]

Stalin and the Moscow bureaucracy saw these Ukrainian national aspirations as the most dangerous obstacle to rebuilding and maintaining Russian domination. In order to crush them, in the 1930s Stalin condemned millions of Ukrainian peasants to death by famine, exterminated almost all the creative intelligentsia, and destroyed the Ukrainian Bolshevik Party and state apparatuses by police terror.

However, this massive terror, of an extent rarely seen in history, "has led the toiling masses of the Ukraine, to an even greater degree than the masses of Great Russia, to look upon the rule of the Kremlin as monstrously oppressive," Trotsky wrote.

The situation today of the local Ukrainian ruling bureaucracy, headed by Volodymyr Shcherbytsky is paradoxical. Although it is resisting the central authorities' Gorbachevite course, the latter are leaving it a lot of leeway, because it is rendering them an important service. It is keeping a heavy lid on the potential for national ferment in the major non-Russian republic of the U.S.S.R.

National Fight Is Spreading

This year the people in the small Armenian republic engaged in gigantic mass mobilizations. On Aug. 23, 1988, the anniversary of the Stalin-Hitler Pact, hundreds of thousands of people in the still smaller Baltic republics went into the streets to demand the historic truth, political

---

Zbigniew Kowalewski, former leader of Solidarnosc in the city of Lodz, is the author of Give Us Back Our Factories: Solidarnosc and the Struggle for Workers' Self-Management in Poland.

democracy, and national freedom. Imagine what would happen if national mobilizations assumed proportional dimensions in the Ukraine.

The fight in defense of the national language and culture, as well as the struggle against nuclear power inspired by the Chernobyl disaster and the battle for the truth about the national holocaust of the 1930s, are spreading to broader and broader social strata. But these struggles are running up against tenacious resistance.[2]

The weakest link in the bureaucratic system in the republic—and it is one of the weakest links in the U.S.S.R.—is the western part of Ukraine. Annexed in the same circumstances as the Baltic countries, the Kremlin fought hard to subjugate it.

Under the Nazi occupation, the Organization of Ukrainian Nationalists (OUN) built up an armed force of 40,000 fighters to resist German imperialism. Once the war was over, the Ukrainian Insurgent Army (UPA) waged an armed struggle and carried on determined underground activity, which was crushed only at the beginning of the 1950s.

However, those years of state terrorism on a grand scale did not break the spirit of the masses. Their passive resistance, as soon as Stalin was dead, led to the Moscow-appointed governor being ousted by the national bureaucracy, which for the first time put one of its own into the post of chief of the republic.

The nationalist fighters, who lost the battle in their lands, mounted a surprise attack from the rear. Having filled the "Gulag Archipelago" in 1953 and 1954, they launched multinational mass strikes in the concentration camps, from Norilsk and Vorkuta north of the Arctic Circle to Kinguir in central Kazakhstan.[3]

German prisoners released from Vorkuta testified: "They say that their program is democratic, that they do not want the return of the landlords and the capitalists. They want only one thing—the Ukraine's independence. . . . Their program very much resembles a socialist program—they say that they are against the existence of classes, and that in this respect the Ukrainian people are different from the Russian people, which has its magnates in the Kremlin."

Heated Up Quickly

It was foreseeable that if anything got started in these lands of an indomitable people, it would heat up very quickly. That is exactly what happened in the summer of 1988 in Lviv, the historic capital of western Ukraine.[4]

The first slogan that took hold among the masses called for democratic election of delegates to the all-Union conference of the Communist Party of the Soviet Union (CPSU) summoned by Gorbachev.

On June 21, 1988, a crowd of 50,000 people tried to intervene in this process. On July 7, over 20,000 inhabitants of the city came out into the streets. On Aug. 4, after the spontaneous street demonstrations had been banned by the Supreme Soviet of the U.S.S.R., a subsequent demonstration was the object of extremely brutal repression by the police, who loosed police dogs on the crowd.

"The sounds of barking dogs, the cries of children, and the screams of women should be the last details of a film called, 'Democracy and Restructuring Lviv-style,'" a statement of the Ukrainian Helsinki Union said.

"The first drops of blood were shed on Lviv streets on Aug. 4, 1988, together with the last illusions of the people of Lviv, whom the ruling apparatus treated as enemies. All was in its place: The people tried to exert their lawful rights—the ruling apparatus responded with repression. . . . It remains to be seen what the second stage will bring."

Leaflets circulating in Lviv proclaimed: "The Stalinists have declared a pitiless war on us. Down with 'the democracy of police dogs,' down with the dictatorship and the violence of the bureaucrats!"

The tone of the demonstrations was set by Bohdan Horyn, a Helsinki Union activist, who described the entire history of the Soviet Union from 1929 to the rise of Gorbachev as "counterrevolutionary and anti-Soviet." He demanded the elimination of the bureaucracy's privileges, the expropriation of the enormous property of the KGB and its diversion to socially useful projects, and the granting of real state powers to the institutions of the republics.

New Mass Front Formed

In the midst of the demonstrations, the Democratic Front in Support of Perestroika was formed, bringing together the Helsinki Union, the discussion clubs, along with the peace, environmentalist and cultural groups (including Jewish ones), among others.

The Democratic Front was also joined by the supporters of the rights of the Ukrainian Catholic Church, which survives underground and has a broad social base.

The initiative committee for the mass mobilizations was presided over by Ivan Makar, a young engineer from the Ukrainian Academy of Sciences. In his fiery speeches, Makar hurled a sharp challenge at the bureaucracy. Besides threatening to call a general strike in the city if the demonstrations were repressed, he demanded that the guerrillas of the UPA be recognized as anti-Stalinist fighters and that monuments be erected to their memory.

Immediately, the Communist Party and the KGB apparatuses ordered the press to open fire and to focus on Makar. He was accused of wanting to rehabilitate the worst "criminal enemies of the people" and of trying to make the region into another Nagorno-Karabakh, a reference to the agitated Armenian enclave in Azerbaidjan.

But Makar was not intimidated by the media campaign. The horrible crimes that were committed in the Ukraine in the 1940s, he said, were the work of the Soviet security forces. All that was necessary to see this and to identify the guilty ones was to open up the archives that have been kept secret to this day.

Makar said: "Walking the streets of our city, sporting medals on their chests, are no few of those who perpetrated real crimes against humanity. They are those who fought not at the fronts of the war but against a peaceful population, shooting people and deporting people to Siberia. They are not saying out loud the whole truth about their 'heroic acts' on our lands.

"They are part of those 'fighters of the Stalinist phalanx' who are always ready, without being asked, to 'offer fraternal aid' and 'liberate' people (robbing them if necessary of the last crust of bread and even their lives), to 'raise' the level of the culture of others and introduce 'limited contingents' into foreign territories."

Portrayed by the official press as an outsider in the service of foreign powers and a self-proclaimed ringleader of the masses, Makar replied:

"It is true that I do not belong to the 'comrades' because I live in a workers' hostel, in a 12-square-meter space that I share with another person. I don't have an official car at my disposal.

"I don't get treatment in the special medical centers reserved for the party regional committee, nor do they send me food at home. I live from a wage. That is my 'trough,' to use your picturesque expression (because you suggest that all of us are feeding out of the 'troughs' of the CIA and similar Western institutions)."

Makar has been jailed, thus becoming the Ukrainian *perestroika's* first political prisoner.

Vanguard of Mobilizations

In the vanguard of the mobilizations has been the Ukrainian Helsinki Union (UHS). This organization was smashed by the KGB at the end of the 1970s. In the mid-1980s, it lost several of its activists in what is known as the Perm "death camp." Among them was a brilliant poet and admirer of the struggle of Solidarnosc, Vasyl Stus.

In March 1988 the UHS revived. In June, it organized a conference in Lviv. Together with dissident groups in Armenia, Georgia, Estonia, Latvia, and Lithuania, it established the Coordinating Committee of the Patriotic Movements of the Peoples of the U.S.S.R.

The statement of principles of the UHS published in July was surprisingly radical in comparison with the positions of similar dissident organizations in Eastern Europe.

Centering on the defense of the right to self-determination of the oppressed nationalities in the U.S.S.R., the UHS considers that its task is to "activate" the popular masses in all areas, with the aim of forming mechanisms of popular participation in the exercise of state power and in real supervision of the state apparatus.

It continues: "For a genuine democratization of Soviet society, limited changes are not enough. It is necessary to break up the existing state system. . . . The UHS calls for the transfer of real power in the republic from the hands of the Communist Party to soviets of democratically elected people's delegates. . . . All parties, unions and informal associations, and even simple citizens' initiative groups must have the right to run candidates for deputies." Trade-union freedom was also indispensable.

The demand for deep-going political democracy was accompanied by the call for deep-going national democracy. On both levels, the UHS proclaimed, "It is essential to abolish completely the antidemocratic, centralist, Stalinist, and Brezhnevist constitutions of the U.S.S.R. and draw up constitutions for the U.S.S.R. and the republics on a new basis.

"In the future, in our opinion, the nations of the U.S.S.R. will be able to live together in the framework of a confederation of independent states. A stepping stone to this may be the formation of a federation of sovereign democratic republics."

The rights of national minorities living in the Ukraine had to be guaranteed by establishing their national-territorial autonomy, and in cases where they did not live in compact territories, through national-cultural autonomy.

The deported Tartars had to be allowed to return to their native land, the Crimea, and re-establish the autonomous republic abolished by Stalin.

Continuity of Historical Memory

The radicalism of the UHS is amply explained not only by the Ukraine's great traditions of national resistance but also by the continuity of the historical memory passed on in an unbroken way from generation to generation of fighters for freedom.

Alongside young activists such as Makar are older dissidents like Vyacheslav Chornovil, Iryna Kalynets, the brothers Mykhailo and Bohdan Horyn, and many others. Sent to the Gulag Archipelago in the 1960s and 1970s, they met activists of the nationalist old guard who fought arms in hand in the ranks of the UPA and later organized the strikes in the forced labor camps.

The UPA's strategy called for "toppling the dictatorship of the parasitic class of Stalinist magnates and the destruction of the Great Russian prison of the nations" through "an all-union social revolution, combined with national revolutions by the oppressed nationalities." On the ruins of Russian domination, the UPA aspired to establish a system of free national states.

The independent Ukraine was to be a people's democratic republic governed by a democratically elected people's power and guaranteed by respect for human and civic rights, political pluralism, and trade-union freedom.

In the free state would be built a "classless society," defined as "a society of workers, peasants and intellectual workers without capitalists, landlords and Stalinist parasites." The foundation would be social ownership of the basic means of production, workers' participation in the management of the production processes and a planned economy.[5]

With respect to this, the program of the Ukrainian Helsinki Union represents a step backward. It supports the so-called "market economy values" that today characterize the "dominant ideology" both of the reform sections of the bureaucracy and the democratic oppositions in the U.S.S.R. and in the Soviet bloc. "To stimulate the economic prosperity of the republic," the UHS states, "[we] consider it indispensable to give the maximum encouragement to private initiative, which can be expressed in the conversion of a part of the state industrial plants into stock companies or cooperatives. . . . What must dominate is a market economy, with its mechanism for freely setting prices. . . ."

The authors of the program do not realize that at the same time they are demanding altogether just and absolutely necessary measures for eliminating the gigantic social inequalities that mark Soviet society, they are proposing the introduction of other mechanisms that generate no less grave inequalities. But it is not only on this ground that the authors of the UHS program are retreating from the best traditions of Ukrainian revolutionary nationalism.

Vyacheslav Chornovil, the leader of the UHS and one of the most outstanding Ukrainian dissidents, has put forward a thesis on the nationalities question in the U.S.S.R. In it he states that the roots of the national oppression established by the Stalinist system have to be sought in Marxist theory itself.

Chornovil states: "One of the weakest areas of Marxism is the theory that the nation is a unity which arose under capitalism, the premise about the total subordination of national interests to class interests, [and] the prognosis not only of a classless but also of a nationless society in communism. . . .

"It is Marxism which produced the infamous 'theory about the fusion of nations' at some unspecified time in the future ('fusion', 'total unity', 'a single Soviet people'); it has been adopted in various versions by all programs of the CPSU and has caused much damage—for without waiting for the 'future' it is being carried out today. . . . Stalin's solution to the national question was definitely not a deviation from Marxist-Leninist theory . . . it was just carried out with inhuman and despotic methods."

According to Chornovil, the definition of nations developed by Stalin in 1913 was the crystallization of Marxist thought in this area. Inasmuch as Stalin's definition maintained that there were no nations not characterized by territorial unity, the Soviet regime could deny the existence of nationalities such as the Crimean Tartars and many others that were expelled from their lands by Stalin.

Chornovil considers that "Lenin began as an orthodox Marxist for whom the national question was of secondary importance and subordinate." He argues that Lenin had to revise his orthodoxy under the pressure of the acute national question that existed in the Czarist empire, and work out his theses on the right of nations to self-determination.

But in reality, Chornovil states, Lenin defended "the inexpediency of self-determination vis-a-vis communist interest (unity of class interest, advantage of larger states in building up socialism)."

At the same time, however, Chornovil pays homage to the proposals on the nationalities question that Lenin presented in his testament in opposition to the great-power chauvinism that was growing at the time. He writes:

"The first steps taken by the national movements during Russia's revolutionary years and also the growth of national liberation movements in the whole world forced Lenin to rethink his own centralistic concepts, he began drawing up a new nationalities policy. . . .

"Lenin even thought that the dissolution of the united socialist state was possible and that the union of independent Soviet republics should be preserved only in the military and diplomatic fields. Unfortunately

Lenin did not have enough time to elaborate his new nationalities policy, and the article mentioned above was concealed from the people up to 1956 and still kept secret later on."[6]

A Position Rooted in Marxism

It does not require much effort to demonstrate the complete absurdity of the thesis according to which the origin of national oppression by the Great Russian Stalinist bureaucracy is rooted in some definition of Marxist theory.

I need only recall that in the Ukraine itself, for more than two decades, various rival Marxist tendencies confronted each other in sharp ideological struggles around the national question and the solution to it.

From 1918 on, within the Bolshevik Party itself as well as within parallel Communist parties outside it tendencies arose on the basis of Marxist theory that tenaciously defended the idea of an independent socialist Ukrainian state. A non-Bolshevik pro-independence Ukrainian Communist Party existed legally in the U.S.S.R. up until 1925, although its founders had resisted the advance of the Red Army in the Ukraine arms in hand.

In the second half of the 1920s, a powerful radical current in the Bolshevik Party in the Ukraine defended national rights against the chauvinist degeneration of the Russian revolution. Its most outspoken representative was the writer Mykola Khvylovy, a convinced Marxist, who called for Ukrainian national independence as a means of resisting this degeneration, which he denounced with all the power of his extraordinary talent.[7]

Among the most radical spokespersons for national rights, including advocates of separation, there were always many Marxists. And many of them were in the vanguard of the successive processes of Ukrainian national revival.

In the mid-1960s, Dzyuba, a Marxist, was the most militant public defender of the national rights of the Ukrainian people.[8]

Revolutionary Nationalists

The Ukrainian revolutionary nationalists of the 1940s who rejected Marxist theory, at the same time opposed equating it with Stalinism. They thought that in order to orient correctly the course of the revolution in the U.S.S.R. it was essential to demonstrate that the Stalinist regime had in fact broken all ties with Marxism, and that it feared genuine Marxism like the devil fears holy water. They denounced Stalin's reactionary theories about building socialism in one country based on the Russian nation as "the leading, preeminent nation."

They recognized that Marxism was the theory that made it possible to show that socialism had not been built in the U.S.S.R. and to unmask the antisocialist, oppressive, and exploitative character of the dictatorship of the Stalinist parasites.

UPA commander Osyp Diakiv-Hornovy wrote: "It is becoming more and more difficult for the Stalinist masters to manipulate Marxism because it is precisely Marxism which is the theory that constitutes their most dangerous foe, for it is completely at odds with . . . and unmasks their policies. Today Marxism looms up equally as a danger for Bolshevism as once it was for Czarism."

"Soviet Patriotism"

Commander Yakiv Busel, another leader of the Ukrainian liberation movement of the time, explained that Stalinism was not a product of Marxism but of a process of great-power chauvinist degeneration of the Russian revolution. He wrote:

"The slope on which Bolshevik propaganda has slipped since the emergence of the Soviet state goes from the ideas of world revolution, which raised the proletariat to the rank of the dominant force in international political life, to ideas of the nation and fatherland, holding that patriotism 'has become the decisive force in the development of the society.' This slope is a reflection of another that goes from the idea of building a world workers' state to that of building a Russian empire."

The "Soviet patriotism" promoted by the ruling clique in the Kremlin, Busel wrote, "is in no way different from bourgeois patriotism—to the contrary it is identical to the official patriotism of every multinational imperialist state."

"Marx said that the workers have no fatherland. Convinced that the workers would win simultaneously in all countries, Marx looked toward a future world workers' state, or more precisely, a future world society. He did not foresee that this society would have special corners or any 'holy lands'. . . . Contemporary soviet patriotism has nothing to do with Marxism. It is the product of a new Bolshevik empire."

Trotsky's Genuine Marxism

The struggle for national and social liberation in the U.S.S.R. cannot be waged effectively if Stalinism is equated with Marxism, if the extraordinary explosive force that lies in the contradiction between them is not understood. That was the conviction of the UPA commanders.

Today this idea retains all its validity.

In one of his last messages, Leon Trotsky clearly defined the fundamental difference between the Stalinists and real Marxists with respect to the Ukrainian question.

The position of the Stalinists, according to Trotsky, was the following: "Inasmuch as the socialist revolution has solved the national question, it is your duty to be happy in the U.S.S.R and to renounce all thought of separatism (or face the firing squad)."

But what Marxists had to say to the Ukrainian people, Trotsky believed, was this: "Of importance to me is your attitude toward your national destiny and not the 'socialistic' sophistries of the Kremlin police; I will support your struggle."

Trotsky explained also that the advanced workers of Russia and the world "must even now understand the causes for Ukrainian separatism, as well as the latent power and historical lawfulness behind it, and they must without any reservation declare to the Ukrainian people that they are ready to support with all their might the slogan of an independent Soviet Ukraine in a joint struggle against the autocratic bureaucracy and against imperialism."9

It is important that the freedom fighters who are taking the lead today in the mass national movements in the Ukraine and other republics of the U.S.S.R. understand that this is the only genuine Marxism.

NOTES

1. Leon Trotsky, *Writings: 1938-39* (New York: Pathfinder Press, 1974), pp. 302-303.
2. More news about these developments can be found in the magazines *Soviet Ukrainian Affairs* and *Soviet Nationality Survey;* as well as in the bulletins of the Ukrainian Press Agency. The address of all these publications is 78B Kensington Park Road, London W11 2PL, England.
3. One Ukrainian leader of the strike in Norilsk published his memoirs. See D. Shumuk, *Life Sentence: Memoirs of a Ukrainian Prisoner* (Edmonton: Canadian Institute of Ukrainian Studies/CIUS, 1984).
4. Lviv is the Ukrainian spelling for Lvov.
5. See A. Wilkins, "Revolutionary Nationalism and Anti-Bureaucratic Revolution," *International Viewpoint*, No. 73, April 8, 1985.
6. V. Chornovil, "Topics for Discussion in the Area of Nationalities

Policies," *Ukrainian Press Service*, No. 5, 1988, pp. 6-9.
7. Some of his works are available in English. See M. Khvylovy, *The Cultural Renaissance in Ukraine: Polemical Pamphlets, 1925-1926* (Edmonton: CIUS, 1986).
8. See I. Dzyuba, *Internationalism or Russification?* (New York: Monad Press, 1974).
9. Leon Trotsky, *Writings: 1939-40* (New York: Pathfinder Press, 1973), pp. 48, 53.